A
HUNDRED
OPTIONS FOR
SUSTAINABLE
LIFESTYLES

A
HUNDRED
OPTIONS FOR
SUSTAINABLE
LIFESTYLES

Successes via Inventive and Cost-Effective Changes

**BROOK
HAYES**

A HUNDRED OPTIONS FOR SUSTAINABLE LIFESTYLES SUCCESSES VIA INVENTIVE AND COST-EFFECTIVE CHANGES

All Scripture taken from the New King James Version®. Copyright © 1982 by Thomas Nelson. Used by permission. All rights reserved.

iUniverse books may be ordered through booksellers or by contacting:

iUniverse
1663 Liberty Drive
Bloomington, IN 47403
www.iuniverse.com
1-800-Authors (1-800-288-4677)

Because of the dynamic nature of the Internet, any web addresses or links contained in this book may have changed since publication and may no longer be valid. The views expressed in this work are solely those of the author and do not necessarily reflect the views of the publisher, and the publisher hereby disclaims any responsibility for them.

Any people depicted in stock imagery provided by Thinkstock are models, and such images are being used for illustrative purposes only. Certain stock imagery © Thinkstock.

ISBN: 978-1-5320-1966-1 (sc)
ISBN:978-1-5320-1967-8 (e)

Print information available on the last page.

iUniverse rev. date: 03/31/2017

Table of Contents

Complaint Department

Despite areas of safe and enjoyable living in special areas in numerous places, much of the world is unsafe, uncomfortable, and frustrating at best. Besides issues of Toxic Air, Floods, Hurricanes, Earthquakes, Tsunamis, and Fires, we have Wars, Rampant Crime, Famine, and bad health. Other issues involve terrorism, instituted for various specious reasons.

Not often noticed are interactions from rude and obnoxious people. Most of us endure these idiots by the dozens. We are at a crossroads regarding our overall abilities to live in relative peace and comfort. Will we eradicate our environment and/or species? Worse yet, will the minority of immoral and evil people make life miserable for the rest of us to suffer on earth?

Drive or walk around and see pretty houses, nice yards, and attractive streets. A quarter of the population may be overweight, so lack of food should be rare. Some villages have nice shopping and eating areas. Shopping malls are models of design and architecture. Skylines of major cities seem inspiring. Externally many areas seem like places you'd enjoy until you meet the people or deal with congestion plus poor infrastructure.

The general malaise is a case of "psychological dissonance". We see a society with vibrant villages, towns, and cities. We believe that things and events that should be logical and reliable. However many functions and results work out to be both unreasonable and wasteful. What issues may have been experienced in the 18th or 19th centuries still can't be resolved by the year 2017.

New problems have taken the place of many old ones. I spent about 1000 hours in 5 years just dealing with internet and computer issues. Many people waste hundreds or thousand of hours on the commute to work each year. Over 30,000 people die yearly from car, bus, truck, train, and airplane accidents. Over a quarter million of us spend money and hours on health-related problems that the doctors, drugs, and experts make worse or can't fix. Thousands suffer addictions to drugs, alcohol, sex, pills, food, gambling, and other temptations. In Asia, it is estimated that 4,000 people die daily from toxic air issues.

Chance meetings, business and bureaucratic relationships and friendships are often strained or hostile. Doing business can be challenging at best because of fraud, maliciousness, and incompetence. Some bureaucratic monopolies seem costly, marginally useful, or downright evil. Some say variations of our species have been on Earth for 2,000,000 years. So why haven't we solved or figured most problems out yet? Why can't we all be civil and moral?

Things to Work On

Reduce medicine and/or doctor induced deaths and diseases
Change automobiles to reduce accidents,
loss of health, and lives
Change Trains and elevate or tunnel tracks to cut down disasters
Make trucks safer to reduce accidents which may lower costs
Make work places safer to reduce millions of injuries per year
Lower toxic air issues which in many
places saving many lives/day
Clean up oceans with trash areas as big as some countries
Build devices and structures to deal with
coastal flooding worldwide
Make solar structures to hold only 4-7
panels for cheap home energy

Use ground based wind energy with
standard materials and devices
Improve vehicles to run mainly on solar
electricity atop the vehicle
Clean up rivers and produce tap water
safe and pleasant to drink
Grow most food cheaply and in places where space is limited
Find ways to purchase autos, trucks, and other
vehicles at low costs Look for sources of low-
cost furnishings, furniture, and appliances
Reduce and/or eliminate trips to hospitals,
use of drugs, and surgeries
Make more durable structures to handle
floods and other disasters
Live well on 4 workdays/week and less
than $30,000/year earnings
Reduce commute times and unemployment nation-wide
Allow people to travel often, cheaply,
and have memorable events

Historical Perspectives

Five thousand years ago, some historians claimed that Egyptians had equal rights for men, women, and some preferred pets (but not slaves of war occupation, or conquest). However, terrorists, tyrants, and warlords dominated much of the world until the dark ages ended in the year 1600. The few exceptions may have been Pericles' Athens around 490 B.C. which boasted a positive form of democracy until Sparta destroyed it a decade later. In the 13th century, a few people tried to bring about science and morality, to little avail.

Most places endured slavery, mass murder, religious intolerance, and diseases. For the privileged, life under ancient ruler was better than slavery. After the birth of Jesus, his teachings, and resurrection have produced more rational ideas than were taught and practiced earlier.

The Bible's New Testament, Romans 13:8-10, Jesus is quoted: "What is the most important of all commandments? "Love your neighbor as yourself. That is by not doing evil to your neighbor. This is the Letter of the Law". Estimates up to a million Christians were murdered before Constantine outlawed epic slaughter in the local arenas and torture on wooden crosses.

In the Old Testament of The Bible, the key issues involve warnings from prophets explaining to people and societies consequences of not obeying the Ten Commandments. It's the same today. You won't find one person in a thousand who knows and/or practices them completely. Significant numbers of people commit adultery. Others abuse people and animals. Most governments steal in one way or another. Murder and torture are considered normal in many countries or states.

Free enterprise may not be free. Other forms of it could be called Fraud Enterprise, and Forced Enterprise as realities of this world. We need to teach everyone to deal with coercion, incompetence, and ignorance.

The internet can assure success, plus provide references to good sources.

Some Good News

The modern world begins with William Gilbert teaching about magnetism (1600), and Francis Bacon's "Twoo Bookes on The Advancement of Knowledge" published on December 26, 1603(the copy I own). In Bacon's works, he proposes respect for good ideas, advancements in knowledge, science, technology, biology, gerontology, and a rational, kinder world.

Documents such as the Magna Charta (1215), List of Rights (1629 in England), Declaration of Independence (1776), and The Constitution's Bill of Rights (10 articles ratified in 1791) had lists promoting specific aspects of liberty, freedom, and justice.

Herbert Spencer published two of the most valuable books ever: Social Statics (1851) and Education (1861). He is a true founder of Libertarian Philosophy and science in education and practice. The age of enlightenment is only a little over 400 years old, despite many lacks of freedom, plus immorality, evil, and injustice today.

Science & Technology

Most of the ideas and advancements of ancient societies were lost or forgotten from 476 to 1600 A.D. Exceptions included the portions of Islamic Civilizations, Cistercians, and a others who presented scientific ideas in the 8th to13th centuries. However many innovators were imprisoned and mostly ignored. Although Gutenberg, Fust, and Schoeffer began publishing books with movable type (from 1455 to 1470), most books printed with few exceptions were classics in fiction and non-fiction, mystical beliefs, religious topics or stories, or irrational views of the real world until 1600. Astronomy, mechanics, and kinematics were rare finds in the 15th century.

The Industrial Revolution got its start with Cistercian Villages and rudimentary technologies in the 12th to 16th centuries. John Evelyn noted the smoke in London in 1665, and suggested trees be planted then. Water wheels were the preferred source of energy. Solar energy is in a formative, stage. Look forward to more our modern benefits and less pollution.

It required the invention of steam engines, artificial dams, coal and oil-fired furnaces, and other inventions to produce goods at reasonable prices for everyone. However, the use of coal, oil, and gas has created massive amounts of pollution from the 17th century to the present. In some areas of the world, the sky is still seen through smoke and smog. We are ready to use some alternatives that make living easier, cheaper, less toxic and stressful, plus more satisfying in general.

Special Notes

New technologies or improvements on existing ones abound in this book. I made experiments on many of the items suggested. Some of them can be dangerous. The author presents these items with no guarantee of success or safety in your application(s).

* I claim there are at least 100 ways to do the same thing. Doing so successfully is up to you. You are on your own as to how well you apply these ideas.

*It is recommended that enclosures for moving items always be built, or that the lowest part of the device be at least eight feet above the ground, away from people, animals, and other potentially harmful devices.

Wind turbines and any hot solar device should be away from all people. The ideal arrangement for turbines would be to cover them, and cover any openings with protective screens or cages placed over moving parts, plus any electrical connections to and from devices.

Solar panels need to be fastened to fixtures to resist most winds. Pay close attention to tracking devices that could be loosened or leave their location.

Growth structures of all types need to be strong enough to handle winds, especially if yours is higher than ground level.

Any home design can be what you desire. For added strength, bigger sizes of wood, metal, and other materials are suggested. They should meet building codes and structural requirements.

The sizes recommended are based on structures that held up in severe conditions. Metals are preferred to wood or plastics.

Try to have anything you buy already tested for efficiencies. Be sure any generator you buy can be checked for output. If you use two generators, be sure both are checked, one for clockwise rotation, the other counterclockwise, and output. Use a volt-ohm-amp-meter to check outputs.

Introduction

Read the ads about the sales and discounts offered. Can you afford the $800 mattress or $800,000 home? Not likely on $30,000 incomes. For 30 years I paid nearly $10,000 a year to the IRS and stayed in debt of $30-60 thousands per year for that long too. Just think – not a chance to pay the debt back in as many years.

So where are you going to get more money? The top ten percent of our populations have figured this out – leaving 90% of us to scrimp and save.

Just think about all those stores, malls, boutiques, shopping centers at prices way beyond your income level. The parking costs at some areas are enough to keep me out. I haven't paid for parking for 40 years and haven't a plan to pay in the future. Fortunately the thrift store and garage sale parking is free, and items are priced reasonably in most cases. The most I've paid for a shirt in 40 years is $10 on sale, but often half that amount.

The Ideal Scenario for buying services and stuff

Most exchanges of a positive sort demand the following:

*Competition from 6 or more sources with no collusion or fixed pricing

Getting many choices available at low cost, by walking, cycling, and/or public transportation.

If public transportation is used, the routes are easy to use, cheap, and accessible by all with schedules that allow for choice of goods and services.

*The product and/or service is good for you and has few health effects or negative side-effects, based on your personal judgment and preferences.

Costs of these items are not out of range of affordability and convenience.

You find civility, morality, and pleasure in acquiring an object or securing a service with few or no exceptions. Problems are rectified quickly and easily.

The provider(s) are courteous, nice, civil, and rarely say or do anything to annoy you.

You are able to choose as you wish with no undue pressure of any sort.

In cases of special needs, the good or service is familiar with the need, and you feel they are compassionate in the way they offer the good or service.

Any errors or deficiencies are made up, restitution is paid, the seller expresses concern for you continued well-being.

If you are harmed in any way, you are compensated and full restitution is made for any harm you suffer. Losses in time and energies are repaid too.

In cases of any natural or humanly caused disaster, you have options to save yourself from further harm, and be restored to your original health or safety in reasonable time.

If for some reason you need time to pay, the costs of credit are very reasonable and are at the lower 10 percentages of what's available.

You have easy access to rating services that can show or tell you which publicly available options were best for others that used them.

Any rentals you make have a contract that spells out your rights and the rights of the lessee, trustee, and owner or landlord. No one is excluded.

Living on A Fixed or Lower Income

Some of your food and medicines can be bought at discount dollar stores for no more than a dollar, versus the higher prices at most stores. You would be surprised at how many items of value are sold in dollar stores.

Rents in some places are less than $800/month, but may require relocation.

Homes in many places can be bought for cash, or at lower prices than rent per month. You may have to consider relocation, checking to be sure they are safe alternatives.

With judicious care, you can find places safe from natural disasters.

Your energy costs are cheap or free. They are installed at low cost.

You can stay comfortable, typically in ranges from 65 to 80 degrees inside.

Goods and services are available at lower and competitive rates.

Communications such as E-mail, TV, Cable, Satellite, and telephone are offered at low rates or for free.

Medical and health maintenance costs are low or free.

Public services are available and noted by E-mail or phone book.

Water and air are relatively free from toxic issues or poisons.

You can grow your own food easily and cheaply.

Social interactions are mostly enjoyable (if you choose wisely).

Crime and warfare problems are minimal in your general area.

You have chosen a place or two to live, quite safe from many disasters.

The settings can be inspiring, delightful, and convenient in most cases.

Your neighbors are civil, helpful, and compassionate.

Chapter 1

Designing Cheap and Elegant Housing for All

The biggest chunk of cash will go into owning or renting a comfortable place to live. In some places, the side effects are road and rail noise, pollution, obnoxious animals, nasty neighbors, and a list of other issues.

Considering all the open spaces everywhere, you would think quiet and inspiring environments could be a "dime a dozen". Most cities are too crowded and noisy for me, so the suburbs are the idea. For example in Thousand Oaks(T.O.), California, alone, there are 15,000 open acres. You could think that at least a thousand acres could be used for low cost places. The mobile home parks are often avoided because of very restrictive regulations and too many irrational demands.

So let's say by some miracle, T.O. gives up a thousand acres and builds 600 to a thousand square foot homes, most of them one or two-bedroom, and taking up 16 homes per acre. This could hold 64,000 people comfortably, as you shall see.

Trompe d'Oeil Architecture

This term is French for giving a live illusion in art. The same can be done in homes to provide the real and optical reality of more space, similar to what might be found in 3,000 square foot homes. It is quite possible to have a three bedroom, two bath with large kitchen and living room layour taking up no more than 1,000 square feet. You'll see some layouts to prove that.

I have watched at least 25,000 shows on TV about home design, and find most people are picky about the wrong things, but if that's what they want, let's give them a lot of it. In other cases there are basics that everyone seems to demand, that homes should offer. With that in mind, I'll list a few things that make both sense and enjoyment.

Lists by Location

Kitchens, the last bastions of disorder and time wastes

All kitchens must have at least a five by five feet space in the middle for two people to work. If there is to be a center table, the area around the table must be at least 3 feet on all sides, with seating on all sides.

There should be a table where two cooks and at least four more persons can sit(including the cook(s), preferably near burners, grill, and barbeque with access to a patio.

Avoid wastes of time (ZVW - Zero Value Work): put two dish-washers in every kitchen, one for dirty, and one to retrieve clean dishes. This addition would eliminate most time wasted stacking plates and stuff.

Put in a refrigerator with counter space, close to a garage to move groceries in, and trash out easily. Place it close to sink for cleaning fruits and veggies.

Open the kitchen to dining area and the living room.

Always have a double sink, and put it close to cooking and serving areas.

Bathrooms That Make Sense and Use

If you come home from work or play, where do you put your dirty clothes? In the washing machine, you can mix clothing and use only cold water.

Your shower and commode should be placed to be handy for people in wheel chairs or who are disabled.

Make your tub and shower have easy access, with handrails or counters to hold while stepping into each one.

Try to have two sinks and a place to work in between them.

Make a place near the sinks and vanities to store stuff, yet close it to avoid a lot of items on the counter.

Make the surfaces easy to clean by not having grout or other places for germs to find a haven. Make the surfaces germ and spill-proof.

Put in commodes that avoid smells and exhaust cleanly out of the walls.

LAYOUT SHOWING 30 AND 24 FOOT LONG CLOSETS

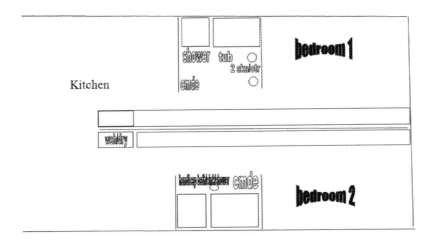

Kitchen

Protected Areas For Sleeping, Storage, Bathroom Access

Have two bedroom walls to allow for two windows that provide air flow that provides fresh and clean air.

The two long closets can be strengthened with 4x4's of wood or iron to be used as protection in storms. Just across from the kitchen can be the pantry. Note that the other side can be used for dining and work on clothing that has been washed and dried.

Have a pair of night stands with drawers to keep the room orderly.

Pick colors that are restful, not reds, yellows, and vivid colors.

A Spacious and Flexible Living Room

It would be nice to have space for showing pictures or TV shows, an exercise room, library, pool room, or whatever – use this room instead.

The smallest living area should be 24 by 16 feet, and no less. Half your home should encompass this space. The kitchen should be 12 x 8 feet.

The net result of kitchen and living room should be no less than 500 square feet with a lot of wall space. Most people feel cramped with any less area.

Use a custom and large cabinet to hide the audio, music, and television.

If you must have an office, put it in the dining area to keep the living area open and uncluttered.

Make the ceilings rise like a "cathederal" or be at least twelve feet high in the center of the closets. There must be a space that is orderly and open and suitable for visitors.

* Make the patio with five concave gables or sides to hold solar panels. The top of the patio would be about 12 feet on sides for 8 feet at the bottom to hold 5 to 10 panels. The cover is about 16 x 6 feet in area. These would be non-tracking panels, fixed to a roof of a different design than normal.

Patios and Courtyard

I'm very much opposed to multi – story homes, and places without patios, terraces, and an outdoor cooking and group meeting space.

*All steps are inherently dangerous, or at best – annoying. Use ramps instead.

The homes of the future will have covers in places too hot or cold to allow swimming, basketball, tennis, running, or other leisure and exercise areas.

Courtyards for 4 to 8 homes are the most economical use of space and utility. They can take away the need for monthly home owner fees and energy costs, if designed properly.

A good courtyard can also be used to grow food and materials for use.

Courtyard Communities

The challenges of these communities deal with people issues, crimes, annoyances, and noise.

There should be some written agreement as to times, activities, and choices of stuff to occupy the area.

Before purchases, there should be some opportunities to meet the neighbors.

The homes around the courtyard should have walls, windows, and doors nearly sound-proof.

Most villages and cities could profitably run the utilities, trash, water, and other services in these communities at low costs with good value.

Hot Tip: set up times and areas for the most favored activities of the group. Avoid noises between 11PM and 7 AM most days.

Some Designs That Fit Future Needs and Uses

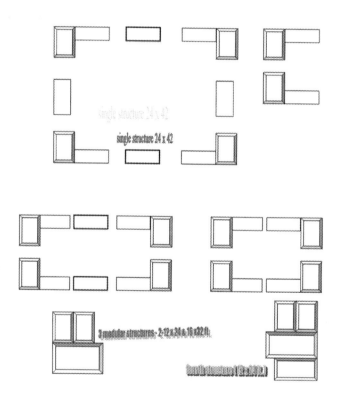

A courtyard community could have from 4 to 8 homes in a group around an open space. Keeping most homes from 960 to 1,400 square feet should be expected. The goal should be to have at least 16 homes per acre including roads and alleys. Larger numbers of homes in the courtyard might not work because of the difficulty in finding enough people who can live together so close and peaceably.

Modular Construction:

Cheap yet quality construction is possible in factories and on the site with proper materials and work practices.

For example, two structures of 12 x 24 feet, and one of 16 x 32 feet could be made as exteriors and laid out as shown above. A larger structure would use a fourth of 12 x 24 feet to extend the living room and/or add another bedroom and bath. The roof lines should be made to fasten easily and not require any objects going through the roof.

The commodes, washer, and dryer should be placed near the outer walls to facilitate drains and air exhausts going through walls (not roof or floor).

The bedroom closets should be made to act as stability for the bed and bat modules, plus storage.

The "L - shaped" construction allows the kitchen to be in two places and accessible to the outdoor courtyard.

There should be four by six inch sized posts spaced every four feet instead of the typical two by fours in present construction. The 4x6's are more than 20 times as strong, and can be better utilized as frames for windows.

For tornado and hurricane areas, the four by fours should be replaced with two to four inch steel I – Beams, placed every four feet, with the beams set in concrete footings, inside Sonotubes with steel rebar reinforcement.

The roof should be made of at least one inch thick plywood sheets (4 foot by 8 feet for strength) with shingles, or with plywood covered with steel or aluminum roofing for protection in fire or wind damage areas.

It has been proven that 3/8 inch thick steel plates can protect against flying debris in most cases. Use the same type of sheets on the lower four feet exterior wall (as "shear walls") for fire and wind protection.

Most access doors should be at least 3 feet wide. This allows for moving furnishings in and out without removing the doors. It also provides easy entry and exit for persons using wheelchairs or mobility devices.

Wheel chair access to the shower should is designed so that no other human is needed to support the person. There should be wheel chair access to the shower and commode in at least one bathroom out of two or three in a home.

Construction Tips

In the case of four inch I beams, the same method should be used. In all cases the vertical beams should not be cut or drilled with holes in them.

The only exceptions would be small holes for screws to hold the wood or steel panels in the exterior or interior walls. Find a strong glue instead.

If there is to be a foundation, never put any pipes or other utilities in it. Check with authorities as to type of footings required for the posts.

The roof should never have any skylight, exhaust, ventilator, opening for air conditioning, swamp cooler, or anything else. Allow for solar panels atop what would be a five gable roof. The top gable is to be parallel with the ground. Let the unit face East to

West for best solar panels for at least 24 feet in length. Each gable should be three or five feet in width to hold the width or length of one or more panels. The ideal exhaust and external lighting would be above the door levels, through the one foot, four inch panels placed above the doors.

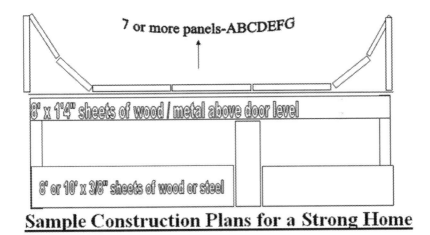

Sample Construction Plans for a Strong Home

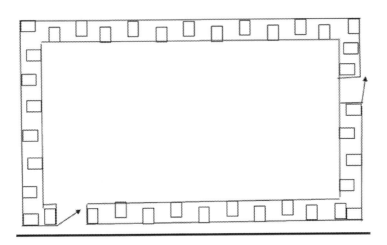

Sample Construction Plans for a Strong Home

Notes:

*Depending on building codes, the four-by-six posts are placed at two or four foot intervals. All doors are at least 6 feet, eight inches in height, so the utilities could be run above the doors to avoid cuts or holes in posts.

The four by sixes should be spaced so that all electrical, plumbing, special wiring, and other utilities run in between the open spaces. These spaces should have at least two inches of open spaces to do this.

Chapter 2

Growing Enough Good
Food For Everyone

Complaint Dept. (again)

It's claimed that the government(s) own about 70 percent of the land in the USA. I drive across the country and notice thousands of trees lying on the ground for the picking. We hear of many fires that waste millions of acres. Why can't we use some of this area for food to feed the world? There's enough wood on the ground to harvest, and usable area to grow lots of useful stuff. You might find this hard to believe, but there is no need to cut trees down for any reason in these government owned areas.

Few folks remember or know of the "mini-ice age" circa 1816. Hundreds of thousands of people died because of the cold and lack of food. A sudden icy condition could wipe out much of the citrus and vegetable production today.

We also have proof that the drought of 1276 to 1296 forced many people in the Southwest United States to move near Montana and Idaho to abandon their livelihoods and homes. It seems that extreme weather can still cause havoc with water and food supplies.

Less Land With Trees and Growing Modules

We may not have the luxury of using billions of acres to grow things. Increased populations result in millions of acres destroyed by suburban developments and removed trees and bushes. In 60 years, the world of 2 billions has gone to 6-7 billion people. If we triple the population by 2072, we will have over 18 billion people occupying large tracts of land. We have to find a way to feed more people with less space, water, energy and resources.

Trees are the skyscrapers of the plant kingdom. It is likely that a potato tree 10 meters high would provide up to a hundred times the produce than those plots in the ground. It also seems that the few ears of corn on 3 meter high stalks would grow more if we could have a few hundred ears sprouting from a 10 meter high tree.

A special pot that hangs and can hold a dozen or two strawberry bushes has been popular in Mexico and Central America. It has various openings that allow many plants to flourish. With larger units, those spacious areas of strawberry fields could be replaced by ten to 100 of those pots in a small area.

Look for boxes with fixtures with openings to grow many plants in 500 square feet ground space. Presently, it seems that there is little need for these modules. After all, a five hundred square foot plot in your back yard could provide enough food for a family. However, as much of the desirable land gets used for housing and businesses. Be sure new buildings have roof or lawn space for useful foods.

The best solution is to go up and put plants closer together. Maybe some four-inch diameter pipes or boxes used to hold a dozen wine bottles could be used. The tropics may have the ideal devices in the form of bamboo, cut to a size to allow plant growth.

In 1984 (Is There A Reef In Your Future? In Waterfront Magazine) I suggested that underwater artificial reefs be used to create waves and grow plants with pipes supporting the rocks to create the waves. The variety of pipe sizes also allowed smaller fish and their populations to be protected from predators. Fish farms with no chemicals are in our immediate future.

The use of fish farms can be made more natural by using pipes or openings in stones to attract and generate varieties of fish habitats. By allowing plants to grow underwater, the farmers won't have to use costly food and materials to get the fish to grow and stay healthy.

Backyard or Front Yard Options

Most people could find four hundred (500) square feet to grow a garden. Other options would allow a small pond to grow fish. Another area could be used to care for chickens for eggs. Trading your labor and time for good food may be helpful if commodity prices increase dramatically. You could keep he space available for the future, despite not using it now.

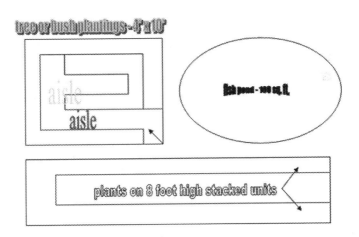

Make your walls add space. In building design, more stuff can be stored on the walls with aisles by the other stuff in the center.

One or more of these diagrams could be implemented in about 400 square feet in your yard.

A Mixed Planting

The typical one type of planting is not suitable on a small scale. In the 1600's the pilgrims could not understand why the indigenous folk had corn that grew better and taller. This was because they planted beans to grow up the corn stalks which fed the earth at the same time they provided food.

It is a known fact that marigolds and other plants help prevent insect diseases and damage to crops when grown with the produce. Check with your nursery or organic websites to find out which plants work well with each other. You might not like broccoli, but you can trade for other stuff.

Some small trees or bushes don't require much water. Try a fig tree or berry bushes to grow your own desserts or stuff suitable for making preserves or jam. Look for desert plants that produce tasty treats without much watering. You may not have the time or water for citrus or other water-intensive plants.

Bell peppers are rich in vitamins and can be put on trellises or tall poles to get the maximum production from them. If you have a few old ladders, use them to support your vines. You will find dozens of types of wonderful fruits and vegetables that will get ample light and space for growth. Keep the height at ten feet or 3 meters at most so you won't have to use ladders to get at the produce.

In some areas, cut two foot lengths of 4 inch diameter pipes and stack them. Place soil in each pipe. The ideal arrangement is to have the open side of the pipes faced 30 degrees up. The diagram shows 96 pipes stacked.

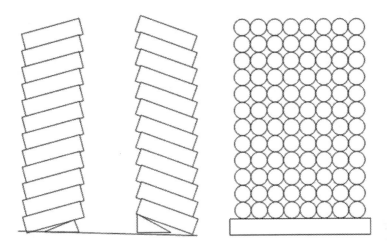

Note that the pipes can be placed facing a central aisle, allowing for 192 different plants to be planted in this small area. Use drip watering above the group of pipes to avoid excessive water usage.

Nutritional Values Not Easily Measured

Nutrition is sort of an unknown factor. It's likely that food benefits vary from one plot of land to another, time of year, and type of compost or growth stimulants added to the soil. Can we really know what foods are giving us the best in vitamins, minerals, and enzymes needed to stay healthy? You might have to err on the excessive side to get what you need.

If you are debating what to grow, you will have to decide which plants will give you the most value and benefits for the space and volume they occupy. It's a little like investing. The experts would have you diversifying – maybe in a few dozen types of sustenance in a small area. Here are 20 basic types of choices you will want to make: Lettuces – Iceberg, Romaine, Spinach, Kale, Bibb, etc. Berries – Strawberries, Blackberries, Acai, Raspberries, etc. Squash – Zucchini, Pumpkin, Italian, Eggplant, etc. Melons – Cantaloupe, Watermelon, Crenshaw, etc. Grapes – white, red, seedless, etc

Tomatoes – grape, beefsteak, Roma, etc.Celery – any type that might be more green than most Figs – Calmyrna or Mission Corn – miniature or regular with tall stalksBeans – green, peas, lentils, black, soybeans, etc.Grasses – wheat, barley, oats, switchgrass, etc. Avocados – Hass or any other typeFlour substitutes – cauliflower, Brussel Sprouts, broccoli, etc.Ground Plants – carrots, potatoes, turnips, radishes, peanuts, etc.Citrus – lemons, limes, oranges, grapefruits in miniature treesTropical – mangoes, bananas, kiwi fruit, papayas, etc Desert – Sapote, cactus, Aloe Vera, etc.Cold Places – apples, iceplant, artichokes, Brussel Sprouts, etc. Protein – almonds, walnuts, chickens or ducks, fish in your pond. Cheeses – milkweed(if safe), soybeans, and new creations plus some dairy with low fat and salt

Stacks and Stacks of Stuff

Take a two by two foot box about six inches high and fill it with soil. Place the boxes so that are stacked about 6 inches apart, and make them about 8 feet high. This will give you approximately 8 boxes for your typical ground grown foods. Try radishes, carrots, potatoes, and other items to see if you can get a reasonable crop in a shallow container.

If you have about 20 square feet of floor (or ground) space, that gives you 5 times 8 boxes, or 40 different options for food to grow in the ground. That could save you a large plot of ground you may not have. If you have a relatively flat roof, try placing the boxes there to get the most sun.

Public Spaces

If you are on the freeway, heading towards Bakersfield (highway 99) note the nice and large and toxic plants in the center of the roadway. Oleanders may look nice, but think of what that center would be with a few thousand trees that bore fruit and vegetables would do to reduce local hunger and poverty. It's odd that many trees you see in someone's yard aren't picked and used. The food just rots. Maybe we will have a private road company who'd like to sell food at a profit, and at low prices, to show the way.

Why not grow stuff in the local patio, courtyard, park, or wherever you see ornamental plants and trees? You don't have to tell me about the complaints. There's too many bugs, or leaves, or droppings, or rotten stuff, etc. etc... It is possible to grow food and also have ornamental plants. Most people don't have the imagination to try it yet. I like the looks of orange blossoms and the fruit.

There is no reason in this world for anyone, anywhere, to go hungry.

Under Our Thumbs and Ground

If you leave the city, you'd find lots of space under the ground. In cities, too many wires, pipes, and tunnels make using these areas challenging. However get into open spaces, and your options are just a shovel away.

Artificial lighting and scarce water tactics will be used to grow much more food than now. Use 20 feet of curved pipe with each end in the ground, cover with plastic, and here's your hot-house. There are plastics that are so thin and strong today, that make the buildings cheap and sturdy.

Depending on your shovel size and technology, you can grow anything below the ground successfully. You could use a variety of skylights to transfer light from above to the plants, so your energy costs stay low. There are tubes that could be used to light a 400 square foot space easily.

Major advantages of underground spaces involve more temperate and comfortable options in hot or cold areas. Any suburbanite could build a small home and have their 20 square meter plot right next to their kitchen. How convenient could that be to have a door from the kitchen to your underground pantry? At worst case, use your garage as a garden.

Do you live in a place that has space underneath? Instead of parking your car there, plant what you need in that same space. Yes, you may need approvals from your association and bureaucrats. Maybe if they are compassionate, they'll let you grow your own stuff for you and others too.

Chapter 3

Cost Effective Medicine and Preventive Methods for Health

Complaint Issues

With the proliferation of drugs, hospitals, doctors, therapists, and "broken window fix-it experts", what are we to do? Is this the proper direction of health? Will we feed substandard food and drink to people, send them to hospitals, use a lot of labor, then make them unable to function normally in later life?

I challenge you to walk through your favorite supermarket and list the things you usually buy. For me, it's about 4 percent of what is available, if that much. So what, again, is the formula? Is the formula to consider, Garbage in, garbage out? For the masses will we subsist on processed, chemically altered foods? Keeping the food fresh may not be the final word on what health and happiness are to everyone.

In the 1970's, I read 500 books on health and longevity throughout the world. It seemed that the people who lived the longest did not have access to all of the stuff we produce, or the vitamins and minerals and supplements many of us take. I don't have the answers, but am suggesting questions that might be worth considering. This is not medical advice, but continuing a general discussion of what people need, not just want, to have as few diseases and health crises as possible

General Alternatives For Progress

Far from my mind is to deprive people from work. Maybe the work could be more of spas, massage, and healthy eating professionals who keep us out of hospitals and care of the doctors and personnel in institutions. I've watched numerous people deal with Alzheimer's, cancer, Diabetes, Liver diseases, dementia, and Parkinson Diseases. It's no picnic for their spouses, relatives, friends, and caregivers. Our first priorities ought to be to find out what prevents us having these slow and stressful issues.

What Hippocrates may have said, "Let your food and drink be your medicine", makes a lot of sense to me. There seem to be many studies (produced at a rate of about 30,000/year) regarding what keeps us healthy. I'm inclined to choose what I do, first.

Drink wine or multiple distilled spirits (like vodka) once or twice a week
Drink 1-2 cups of coffee and special teas (about 8-16 ounces) daily
Have at least 2 servings of fruit daily
Cook or eat at least 2 servings of vegetables daily
Eat mostly fish, chicken, and pork – fresh and raw (with No nitrites)
Limit beef, ham, bacon, pepperoni, and sausages twice weekly at the most
Barbeque the fish, chicken, pork, and meats in a marinade
Avoid mixing starches and fruit with meats and vegetables
Have fruit for breakfast, with no more than a few eggs weekly, etc.
Try to find sweets that won't have too many processed sugars
Mix plain yogurt with a natural sweetener to lower sugar amounts
Scramble eggs and salsa and cheese to get protein and vitamins
Make cakes with rice or gluten-free flower, oatmeal, and Club Soda
Melt low sugar chocolate, add nut and fruit trail mix, and freeze for candy
Broil and bake most items to avoid fried food
Cook brown rice, and add vegetables in a steamer, and sauces that are fresh

Pay attention to what container foods come in and what you use for cooking

Exercise every other day for at least 20 minutes

Your gym or outdoor exercise program should suit what you like to do.

You will find that a way to enjoy some special form of play or sport will keep you happy. For me it's riding a boogie board in the ocean and walking in a swimming pool, from three times a week or more.

If you want to read what seems to be the best study on what exercises are best, try reading and using the ideas in Kenneth Cooper's Aerobics.

If you have a pool nearby and at low cost, make sure it's water is comfortable and use it as often as you can. Try to stay in it for a half hour, and vary your exercise and play routine. Do stretching and pull exercises too. Having a pool at home is the ultimate luxury, especially if it is out of sight of your neighbors or unwanted visitors.

Judging by how few people occupy pools, lakes, and oceans, I may be in the minority. Part of the problem in many places involves weather that is too extreme. In other cases, you can't leave anything valuable in your vehicle or on the shore. What incentive is there to use these areas?

If you own a home of any sort, try to find a way to put in a pool, Jacuzzi, or other form of entertainment. Why not put in a gymnastic piece or set of equipment? Find some ways to enjoy your yard or patio if available.

Mixing Fun with Eating and Exercise

Most cultures enjoy forms of dancing, music, and sports – maybe all at the same time. Find what suits you and your friends. Look for groups in your area that enjoy all aspects of music and gatherings.

Hopefully you have some form of work or a job. Considering the bosses and managers I worked with, that job can be stressful. We don't seem to have trained managers how to avoid being angry, hostile, or idiotic. It just seems to be part of the business domain. If you work one or more of these creatures, find ways to de-stress outside, or even during work.

Chapter 4

Indestructible Homes at Reasonable Costs

Controversial Complaints (please don't get angry)

Not all places qualify for a cheap and modular home of 1,100 to 1,500 square feet in size. There are many places where the home could fly off like the one in the "Wizard of Oz". In the real world, the process is painful and recovery costly.

What is convenient for contractors may not be so pleasant for the occupants. You may not agree, but it seems that many homes are built for the designer and builder's convenience and profit, and not to keep the residents safe or happy. There are exceptions, but I haven't seen much that's impressive. Why would I waste time on a book if things were so ideal?

Trading Labor for More Expensive Materials

In a televised special, it was noted that 3/8 inch steel plates could protect some vehicles against underground bombs. It just happens that those same plates are heavy, and resist fires well too. Some tropical places have demands for metal roofs that stay on the home in high winds. They also resist catching fire from hot embers from burning plants and trees. Steel is both cheap and very durable. The difficulty involves putting coatings on the steel to avoid rust.

Depending on where you live, wouldn't it be better not to worry about floods, fire, winds, earthquakes, and even bombs? The costs aren't prohibitive if a home is designed for it in the first place.

All this is preamble to what simple changes can be made to build or retrofit a building in dangerous areas. The contractor will complain of higher costs, but some of those can be prevented or alleviated with other technologies offered here. If my friend and I couldn't open a one thousands of an inch thick plastic package without scissors, we can use the same stuff to save ourselves trauma and massive annoyances in structures.

Stick versus Bigger Sticks, I-Beams, Stones, Shear Walls of cast iron

The builders' use of "stick construction" works in places with few risks. In many places it's risky at best. Did you know that a 4 x 4 is 20 times stronger than a 2 x 4 piece of wood of similar material that is 8 to 10 feet long? Many builders swear by a 2 x 6, but I'd opt for the 4 x 6, noting that it will keep the walls narrower and stronger than the 2 x 6 in some cases. Using 4 x 6's lowers labor costs for better frames for windows and doors.

For more dangerous conditions, pick a cast iron or steel 4 x 4 inch tube or I-beam, still keeping the walls less than 8 inches thick. In windy places, concrete footings of 8 cubic feet are a must for each beam, spaced 4 feet apart as in the "post and beam construction". Use of metal I-beam construction could make the building a hundred times as strong.

Most windows should be made of one quarter inch thick(never less than that) bullet-proof glass or plastics for better protection and insulation. A developer building a hundred homes does not like to read this, but they rarely have to deal with thieves or objects blown in the wind.

Trading lower labor rates for more expensive materials could mean a better life for many home owners. Most of the complex methods to get windows and doors put in homes could stop with better and straighter wood or metal.

In a 1918 handbook, it is suggested that concrete blocks (about 14 inches long by 8 inches wide) can be laid down side to side instead of end to end. This results in about 60 percent more blocks being needed for the walls. However, this also results in a much stronger building with 60 percent better insulation.

The obvious objections involve added number of bricks, cost, labor, and materials. A longer term and more customer – oriented philosophy would prove that this is a much better design for many buildings, saving energy and likely lives in case of earthquakes, winds, and floods.

Floor and Utilities Issues

Some surveys claim and heating and cooling losses can be as much as 30 percent with a concrete slab as a floor. The other major issue involves floods that will destroy or damage the electrical, plumbing, air conditioning, and other utilities. In my tours of the Gulf Coast after Hurricanes Ike and Katrina, it seemed that some buildings survived, but most utilities were destroyed, rendering living there useless.

A two foot high electrical plug is useless in a 4 foot flood in a home. Some wind that blows sand and dirt into an air conditioner makes heating and cooling costly or non-existent for awhile. What may have been cheapest to sell the unit becomes costly to the inhabitants suffering a disaster.

One of the pleasures of being in a home built by Frank Lloyd Wright was the indirect lighting coming from the ceiling. To me, it was a hallmark of his many ideas for innovative designs. Carried further, we might want to consider having most or all utilities located near the ceiling. For many electrical devices, the wireless transmitter controlled by remote control would allow many devices to be powered and controlled from above.

Today, small plastic pipes and tubing are replacing the costly iron and copper pipes of the past. The water supply could come from above, and the only the drains still could be placed below the floor. As discussed earlier, all outward air exhausts should always be out of a window or wall, never the roof.

To keep comfortable, we might want to consider tubes of oil heated or cooled placed near the floor. The traditional floor coverings would still be available – carpet, wood or laminate planks, and tiles. Heating and cooling the floor would remove the losses usually experienced in present home construction. Most homes should be built on footings with wood or iron columns, anyway. In fire-prone areas use 3/8 inch thick cast iron panels.

The days of on-site home construction are numbered. Modular and a fixed mobile home system from the factory will be normal. I already have quotes from a few builders for homes costing $50,000 or less, at $40 a square foot. Most homes today cost from $200 to $400 a square foot to build.

The most expensive aspects of building involve plumbing, air conditioning, electrical, and the kitchen. By making the utilities easily placed in a home, these costs will be reduced dramatically. Placing them near the ceiling also reduces the risks of floods everywhere.

The floor should be designed to allow tubing to remain during floods, with the cooling and heating devices on the walls above. Placing utilities in carports or basements is not a good idea, unless you don't mind their destruction in cases of disaster. I can envision floors being made of plastic tubes and openings with the wood or stone veneer on top of the tubes. There are solar panels that hold liquids available now to do just that.

Considering how difficult it can be to open a plastic mail or food container, we could build floor panels and roof panels out of strong and bullet-proof materials. By having the roof materials as tubing, we can heat water by the sun and move it from the roof to the bathroom and kitchen areas.

Forty years ago we installed fiberglass panels used in the food industry for wall panels in various parts of a factory. They proved to easily maintained and nearly indestructible. The polycarbonates of today can fulfill the same needs at lower costs.

Some homes could have these panels that cover all the walls, eliminating the need for windows. Curtains would be used wall coverings for privacy or light-control issues if the plastic is clear. Other buildings might use opaque and clear panels to avoid needs for curtains altogether.

A short note on Sustainability

Why worry about saving trees when they are renewable. In the 1930's, Henry Ford and George Washington Carver designed vehicles to use strictly farm raised materials. They envisioned all plastics and composite materials as the way to build all vehicles. Unfortunately Mr. Carver died, and so did the plans to complete this mission.

What exist in relatively finite and short supply are oil, gas, metals, stones, and rare earth materials. We need another Carver or few more innovators to develop these alternatives before these traditional items are scarce or gone.

Some oil companies already run ads claiming we have enough natural gas to last a hundred years. I've already lived 70 years and observed gasoline prices go from $.29 to $5.00 sooner than I expected. It is likely that waste products from bushes and trees will be our next major sources of energy and materials. A few people in chemical and materials sciences need to work on more final and long-term solutions today.

solar and wind devices can be improved.

I have a few suggestions in later chapters. In Palm Springs, a lot of solar panels could be placed near the wind turbines. After driving through Western Oklahoma, that state has enough area of high winds to power most of our USA.

Many of our cities aren't delightful places to live. Some new methods of making millions of people happy in congested areas must be proposed. Some people should be working on making life in large cities delightful in the context of high density – no easy task. Extreme weather should be ruled out by designs to allow people use of pools, playgrounds, leisure pursuits, and relaxing in all areas of the world. Covered play spaces are a must.

Chapter 5

Designing Decent Roads
to Avoid Accidents

Complaint Department Gridlock

Take a vacation and then drive home through Southern California, and you will know why many people are neurotic and rude. The roads are congested and illogical. Drive on a five lane freeway and then have it squeezed to 3 lanes and plan for gridlock at most hours. What may have been a relaxing visit elsewhere turns into drama and stress if you live within a hundred miles from the center of various large cities.

If you want to find an example of one of the least successful bureaucracies in the world, pick CALTRANS. If the goal is to get from point A to point B with ease and no stress, they get a D in my book. These roads are the worst of the 55 countries I visited over the last 40 years. In February they caused a 4 hour traffic jam in a few hundred yards of road near Palm Springs. They are good a apologizing, but not designing or building roads.

The use of this chapter will remedy most defects in our road systems.

Most of the congestion and accidents were designed into the roads

This chapter will describe a typical problem and the solution. There are certain scientific principles and technologies that apply to all roads. Hopefully in a few hundred years they will be practiced.

You are stuck for a a minute or more at most stop lights

Convert the stop signs to round-abouts for one or two lane roads. You can find good examples in Great Britain and Sedona, Arizona(they involve roundabouts and work much better than most stoplights).

You are stopped or slowed down by a change of the number of lanes

Keep the road at the same number of lanes along the whole freeway or route. Do not reduce the lanes as CALTRANS did on the newly constructed Highway 210 between the 605 and 10 Freeways.

Traffic is backed up when you approach a different freeway on or off ramp.

Add a transition lane at every intersection to or from the other freeway.

Traffic is slowed down while cars get on or off the ramps of the road

Add a transition lane separated by barriers that only allow exits and entry every 3 kilometers or 2 miles of road. The only example of a successful design is on the 710 Freeway from Atlantic Avenue to the 105. It is still the least congested area of all of the LA freeways.

Two or more high occupancy lanes are crossed in the wrong lanes or places increasing congestion

Place barriers along most or all solid double lined portion of the HOV or Diamond Lanes.

Left or right turns block vehicles behind the vehicle making the turn

Prohibit all turns and make the person go around the block without blocking traffic. This should be demanded on Ocean Avenue in Venice, California.

Railroads cause delays in traffic in urban areas

Overpasses or Underpasses are much cheaper to maintain than the complex signals that often are scenes of many accidents. The San Fernando Valley has hosted numerous deaths and accidents from train or signal errors, or the errant humans and/or vehicles on the tracks.

Trains are damaged or destroyed when they hit each other

All train routes must have two separate tracks for traffic going in two directions. Any intersections should have under or over – passes to avoid signaling and accident issues.

Trucks occupy two or more lanes on most roads

Offer trains that carry the whole truck, or create truck roads and lanes for trucks only as is done on the 5 and 405 Freeways near San Fernando, California and the Van Norman Dam.

Large potholes damage vehicles and slow traffic down

All holes should be filled by specialists with liquids that can be poured into the hole that bind successfully with the existing roads, be they asphalt or concrete.

Exit and Entrances are closer than 2 miles apart

Traffic trying to enter and exit in any shorter distance will create gridlock and potential accidents.

Too many exits to roads and freeways are too close

Most drivers are confused by two or more exits to other roads in the same place. They will slow down, and often cause confusion and gridlock. Any exit to anyplace should be more than 2 Kilometers or 2 miles from each other.

"Looky Loo's" are created by accidents, highway patrol vehicles, and other emergencies and/or distractions.

Officers should try to move errant vehicles to sidestreets. The opposite side of the freeway should not be visible to those drivers. Some way of removing unusual vehicles or situations should be attempted.

Ample lanes and distances should be made for schools, stadiums, and major attractions to reduce gridlock

Note the places near colleges, and invariably, gridlock occurs because the road planners did not offer enough lanes to exit, or ample distances to hold the added vehicles. This is obvious near most stadiums where sports are played.

Many attractions are the cause of traffic tie-ups and/or accidents too. Easier access with overhead or underground ramps should be considered and built.

City and local congestion reduced and/or eliminated

In the last 20 years, most places have now become so congested as to take an hour to get 10 miles, if you are lucky. Travel times can vary from 8 to 28 minutes to go 5 miles. You can be reminded that for every minute elapsed, a pound of Carbon Dioxide per car goes into the air. Multiply that by thousands of cars daily, and plan on wearing gas masks sooner than later. Some cities have solved these problems, in Rancho Mirage and Sedona.

All stoplights should be coordinated to allow 25 to 45 mile per hour travel with few or no stops

In Rancho Mirage, California, lights on Highway 111 are set and allow continuous travel at 35 miles per hour. On highway 179 in Sedona, Arizona, roundabouts have improved travel times from 30 minutes to 8 minutes for 5 miles of travel.

Priorities should be set as to the top 20 streets to have and guarantee no stops for much of their distance.

In some areas, the side street traffic may have to wait 2 to 3 minutes to allow this to happen. On rare occasions, I can go from Sunset Boulevard to Malibu Canyon Road with no stops, about 12 miles, on Pacific Coast Highway. In small communities, roundabouts could allow unimpeded travel just by removing the stop signs or lights.

Where possible, each road should have a left, right, and two straight line lanes.

Doesn't it anger you when you sit for 3 minutes because you can't pass the cars on the right to turn right? Even worse it the situation when only one person goes straight, preventing you from turning right? If necessary, a left lane should be eliminated to allow smoother traffic flow. In other places, just relocating utilities could make travel more pleasant.

Fully one-way streets must be considered to allow more vehicles to get from point A to point B in any city

At some time or another, city growth should include more streets that only allow one-way travel. If necessary, overhead lanes and ramps should be considered. This may require added parking structures, or limited times during rush hours for parking and stopped traffic. In some cases, vehicles should only be allowed to make right turns in congested areas, to avoid left turn issues and accidents.

Roundabouts should become the most favored way of traffic style, no light, travel, in less congested areas.

In Florida, 821 citizens sent a letter to avoid having a roundabout built in their area. Despite the 93 page justification that half the injuries and deaths would occur, the locals say keep the stoplight.

There are hundreds of thousands of streets in small cities that would reduce travel times dramatically with roundabouts. They allow people to travel with no stop signs, despite slower speed limits on two-lane roads. I would strongly recommend that any locality questioning the benefits have a qualified observer visit Sedona, Arizona and take videos of the traffic differences using stop lights and roundabouts.

In some places, overhead travel and ramps should be constructed to eliminate need for lights or roundabouts altogether.

This may seem like an extreme measure to allow traffic to flow smoothly. In new cities, or in areas allowing overhead travel, this could be an option to reduce accidents altogether. It would be like having a freeway entrance, exit, and direct travel option in the middle of a congested city.

For places where the railroad operates, with tracks in crowded areas, this should be a major consideration. In the San Fernando Valley, California, a few major overhead intersections would reduce the number of accidents and deaths on a cost-justifiable basis.

Chapter 6

Making most Vehicles Safer and Less Annoying

Complaint Dept Additions

Trains, trucks, cars, vans, etc. kill about 40,000 people a year – or at least those persons driving and suffering. Estimates of 13,000,000 accidents occur yearly in the USA alone.

The "broken – window" promoters would say they are good for business. Frederick Bastiat coined this phrase in the 1840's to emphasize that fixing problems is worse than spending money for desired objects and services. After all, think of all those new cars, parts, roads, and repairs to be made. We have to have these accidents to keep people busy and employed. We kept 10,000,000 people busy during World Wars I and II, yet few of us would want to repeat these events. It is hard to believe a lot of people are unemployed by losses of polio, small-pox, and AIDS in recent years.

What drives people mad or indignant involves how miserable getting from point A to point B is these days. Pick a method and plan for annoyances and stress. In 2009 I drove 7,600 miles across the USA, and worse yet I drove 8,000 in 2015 in the Summer. What distress. Delays were typically two hours/day. I endured at least a dozen near-crisis accidents. I'm not the only one who finds most forms of travel frustrating. I saw very few travelers last Summer on the road.

The Solutions Were Removed or Destroyed Years Ago

Years ago, special bumpers were used by taxi drivers in a few cities that prevented accidents, so they were removed. We used to have a "red-car" transit system in LA, and that was removed. Not too long ago, bumpers were mandated to survive 5 MPH hits, and they were removed. There are a lot of special interests who want to keep us with deaths, accidents, high gas prices, poor gas mileage vehicles, and dangerous roads(despite what they say).

What these people don't realize is that the same money wasted on vehicle and road issues could be used to promote travel, hotel stays, vacation packages, and having more leisure and fun. Removing potholes and guaranteeing reasonable speeds got lost with the so-called new materials and methods in road building. Note the differences in roads on Hwy 10 in Texas. It is obvious that the light colored concrete had fewer cracks and scraps of tires in the tested area.

Why Can't We Make Indestructible Vehicles?

The apologists for all this death and mayhem will tell you we can't put all this new technology into vehicles without excessive costs. They are absolutely wrong. Fifty years ago, the only person who believed privately funded space travel would happen was Andrew J. Galambos. Fifty years from now, we will have a tenth of the accidents we suffer now using fully protected vehicles.

We could make most vehicles safer, but choose not to. It would be easy to design cars with bumpers that will rarely suffer damage. We have materials to keep side panels and doors safe at most speeds. A few vehicles used to have some panels that did not scratch. In one vehicle, I was hit behind by people traveling 40 miles/hour and suffered little vehicle damage of my own. Ceramics and composites are made to handle high temperatures and damages.

Are the police and armed forces the only people who need bullet – proof clothing? How about bullet – proof cars, windows, and bumpers for us all? We might want to resurrect a few "bumper – cars" from the amusement parks to set proper examples. On one TV program, they added a 3/8th inch steel panel to the bottom of a vehicle to keep the occupants safe during a roadside bomb attack. Considering how cheap polycarbonate panels are, we could make a vehicle out of molded plastic. I've already see single panel swimming pools and spas, so vehicles with a few panels would be easy to do.

True Automobiles Drive Themselves

I find it amusing that the so-called automobile is highly labor intensive. If you do not pay attention, you can have an accident "in a New York minute".

In 1967, a prototype self-driving auto was produced for an extra $3000 when my Chevrolet Camaro cost me the same amount. Do you really believe we can't do this? We now have some cruise controls that slow or stop in an emergency, and self-parking cars. Calling all car makers - yes we can make a true automobile now, in 2012.

It's likely that in many car-maker's boardrooms, the plans are there, but to be doled out in piece-meal versions over the next 40 years. Let's do it now and get the driver's role automated ASAP.

Most people failed to notice that in the 1970's, warehouse forklift trucks were designed to move without a driver. At Weiser Lock, in 1980, a system was installed reducing staff from 15 to 3 using these forklifts. The key was a wire laid into the concrete floor. We could do the same on most paved roads. I'm sure Disney has done this already in some of their parks. The New York Times has already automated their lifts for rolls of newspaper stock.

Idiotic Lights

It's amazing how a hundred year old technology of stop lights is so much still of the "dark ages". I used to drive 10 miles in Long Beach and was never stopped in 12 miles. Now the same trip will take an hour if I'm lucky. A recent drive on Rosecrans Avenue from Paramount to El Segundo Beach took 80 minutes for 24 miles, a whopping 20 miles an hour. I was stopped at 100 lights. If this is progress, maybe the horse and buggy is due for a reprise.

In many cities, the lights 100 feet from each other are not timed to allow travel without stops at both lights. I live in a city with nominally 150,000 people, but driving it reminds me of LA congestion with a vengeance. It's obvious that the traffic bureaucracies have no interest in saving people time or gas.

One might think that the most traveled roads would have signals set for a reasonable speed of 35 miles per hour as they do in Rancho Mirage near Palm Springs, California. It's the only stretch of Hwy 111 you can drive with no stops. There never that chance in my area. My trips on Lynn and Olsen Roads to Cal Lutheran College's swimming pool takes from 7 to 24 minutes depending on how many stops are made with the 18 stop lights on my route.

The very first thing I would do in every village, town, city, county, or parish would be to set the stop lights for a reasonable speed on at least 50 percent of the roads in the city, or at least the ones most used.

In Thousand Oaks there are a dozen main roads, and all of them should have the signals set for continuous use and avoidance of stops of any length of time. The left turners and vehicles at intersections should wait.

Many intersections should have the lights removed and underpasses or overpasses constructed, as with train crossings. All train crossings in various cities should have the same constructions. The use of lights and crossing guards in cities costs people lives and accidents.

Chintzy methods to slow you down or make you stop

You are stuck at a signal and you can't turn because they omitted the right or left arrow that could have been put on the light meter stand. It's not that there aren't at least one like this in your city. They just decided not to add it to dozens of intersections.

In the San Fernando Valley and a few thousand other places, congestion is the norm, especially with no left or right turn signals at hundreds of intersections. You often get stuck waiting for three or more complete changes of the lights just to turn left. If it costs so much to put proper signals with timing, why not just eliminate them and place roundabouts at the intersection instead?

The train and bus bureaucrats are no better at rational and cost-effective operations. Many of the costly failures of train travel over the last century have been caused by short term cheap thinking and projects. Instead of putting two tracks side by side, they just use one track, signals, and get lots of accidents and delays instead. Travel across country and you find long trains stopped for minutes or hours because of the single tracks. How can they make a profit if they operate so illogically?

The bus companies are rarely better. While waiting in LA on a bus to La Crescenta, I watched 14 busses headed toward Rimpau St. that were empty in the hour I waited for my bus. A hundred years ago, a concept called linear programming was designed to deal with these issues. It would be unlikely bus travel would be so onerous if this and other operation analysis methods were used to avoid wasted bus travel and trips. Try using science, not just people with a pencil and paper.

Has anyone discovered what timing a bus would need to just go from point A to B, C, D, etc., then back in the same direction, maybe fifteen minutes later(allowing a break for the bus driver)? Let's assume a 45 minute route of 5 to 10 miles, a fifteen minute stop, and then back again, 4 or 5 times for the driver to get his or her 9 hours of work daily, four days per week.

Some aliens from other worlds would be amazed at how many and how wasteful trucks are on our roads. Something is wrong when you see hundreds of trucks taking up two lanes on our roads and freeways most of the weekdays. Has anyone calculated the savings of the Alameda Corridor?

It's a direct truck line from Long Beach to the center of LA. Maybe it would be useful to have these all over the USA, and the world. Considering how much space is lost on the railroads carrying the 53 or 48 foot truck vans, why not carry the whole truck with driver?

Supposedly we have enough natural gas for a hundred years. Someone should get the trucks on this fuel very soon. I see trash trucks promoting their use of natural gas, so it seems the other trucks could all do the same until a better alternative fuel is developed or invented. Costs of conversion are cost-effective at $5/gallon diesel gas costs.

If we had more efficient solar cells, most trucks could be partly electric motor powered. The most obvious energy producing effect would be to have 8 foot by 53 foot roof space on the trailer van in solar cells. At 300 watts/ 15 square foot, that works out to be about 8,000 kilowatts of solar power per hour of sun.

Twenty years ago I sent a letter to an airline suggesting that their services could be more efficient. It seemed that bulk foods and alcohol could save them thousands on each flight. Instead we lost cheap meals altogether with no bulk savings methods.

Airline baggage handling is still in the Stone Age, at best. Hasn't anyone heard of MTM or Methods Times Measurement? It was used by a few industrial engineers until the profession was wiped out by losses in manufacturing jobs in the first decade of the 21st century. Most planes should be designed for carry on luggage of 4 foot long by 3 foot wide by 1 foot deep luggage. The presently small carry on methods are unreasonable and useless for many travelers. With exceptions of larger parcels, no baggage should be handled more than once from the user to the plane, and vice-versa.

Considering the methods available for security, there should be a way to get people through to the airplane in 10 minutes or less in all cases. First of all we should not have people waiting in areas before entering the plane. What a waste of space. A temporary wrist band as used in hospitals should replace the silly papers and tickets. Entries into the plane should be in three places, not just one. All seats should be pre-assigned and entry based on logically filling the seats in order so as to avoid delays inside the airplane. Those who cannot fill their assigned seat should still pay, and have the seats left empty.

Inside, easier methods to secure food and drink would be nice. What about someone with bulk containers filling your plates and glasses or a buffet?

Chapter 7

Getting Your Power Cheaply or "Off the Grid"

If you believe NASA is the only tax supported institution now using private enterprise to solve some transportation issues, you are sorely deluded. You may choose to have sources of energy outside of power grid in the future. In some cases you can make money by supplying energy to others close by.

Gushers All Over The World – 1859 - 2029

Back in 1859, it seemed like oil would gush up forever. Steam and electric powered vehicles could not compete with the new fuel that cost so little. What may have been a nickel a gallon gas a hundred years ago costs from 50 to 100 times that amount.

I traveled 7,600 miles throughout the USA for $400 in 2009. Three years later the same route would triple my cost. If you have 3 people to share the cost, you could travel cheaply. Natural gas is a temporary fix, with claims of another 100 years available for vehicles and energy production. These predictions may have been valid with a 2 billion world population. In 20 years from now, all gas, coal, and oil options may be reserved for the ultra-rich.

"Don't Cry for Me, Argentina" is a favorite tune of mine. You can sing the same tune for oil, coal, and gas in favor of solar, wind, geothermal, and plants. The sooner we make plans for renewable sources of energy, the faster we will guarantee wealth for all humans on Earth and beyond. At least, we should use natural gas, clean coal, and oil as interim measures, not final solutions.

Not Reserved for the Minority or Unconventional People

You wouldn't find me placing a hundred foot tower and a wind turbine in my front yard. Nor would you see a hundred solar panels on my roof either.

Most people agree with me. Wind turbines can be noisy and may kill birds. I spend about $30 a month on electricity and $5 on natural gas. There are many ways to save on energy that still allow you to plug or pipe in your energy source. The first things you can do are to look for ways to lower your energy costs now. This should be your top priority if you wish to live economically and self-sustaining with little help from others.

Pick 25% of your options to save 75%of your power. Besides using low energy lights and Light Emitting Diodes find other ways to save if you use these noted appliances and expect these costs:

Your refrigerator: $2/month
Your grill and burners: $1/month
Your toaster oven and coffee maker: $1/month
An electric heater and a 10,000 BTU window Air Conditioner (in summer without heater in one room: $8/month
A "Swamp Cooler" using water to cool large areas with low humidity: $6/Month
TV: $3/month
Audio: $1/month
Gas Stove: $4/month
Water heater: electric 10 gallon, $5/month
Lighting: $2/month
Total Costs: Probably from $27 to $40/month for an 800 – 1,000 square foot home with 1-2 persons and 1-2 bedrooms.

If you live in extreme climates, these costs will vary, and can be affected by how well your home is insulated as well as having windows and doors open to winds with good air flow.

Planting a few trees and bushes near your windows can provide shade plus lower energy costs significantly. As much as a third of your air conditioning costs come from floors staying too cool with tile and laminate or wood planks. Carpet with thick padding makes better insulation in most places.

If you spend a lot for water, use only cold water for washing. Try washing your hands in cold water too. Get rid of your dryer if you can dry your clothes outside.

Your electrical appliances may be major wastes of energy. Consider miniature items using rechargeable batteries instead of full-sized items. Use a rechargeable phone for your music, internet, purchases, and entertainment. If you still use magnetic tape and compact discs, try the battery and portable devices previously popular. Make sure your refrigerator uses less than $4/ month in energy requirements. The same goes for your washer. Do not use an electric dryer, unless you cannot dry stuff inside or out.

The kitchen is that last bastion of disorder. Consider a microwave, toaster oven, and a couple electric burners for your cooking. You can cook most stuff in a square 12 or 14 inch electric skillet, six quart pot and wok. Be sure you have good lids for these devices. The wok works great for baking too. If you can, buy a ceramic and stainless steel knife for cutting all items. Use cold water with antibacterial soap for cleaning utensils and wares.

Do you live where the sun is often available? Get two thousand feet of black hose at least 5/8 inch diameter and connect it to your water source and home. Set the hose outside to heat water. Do not let rainwater go to waste. You should have a 10,000 gallon pool that can be covered to collect water. When it rains, place tarps along the side to collect water into the pool.

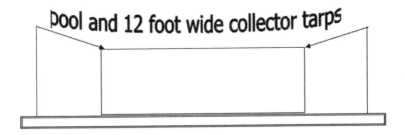

First of all you want to avoid using propane or natural gas to take advantage of using wind or solar electricity. Make some or all of your appliances use 12 volts if you can. Use tablet or small computers with long battery lives. Consider using shavers, toothbrushes, and other small stuff with batteries or hand operated to save money. This way you can use your wind or solar power device for recharging storage batteries instead of running larger motors and hardware.

Try using a 12 to 120 volt inverter for small devices. This way you charge stuff while you travel. Shavers, cell phones. Wireless phones, tablets, and other devices are ideal for use at no cost to you, other than driving.

Less Obtrusive and Costly Wind Power

There is a reason we don't use propellers on planes anymore (with a few exceptions). They are inefficient and don't collect the wind very well. Your cheapest options are large powder cans, kitchen mixer bowls, or 6 inch pipes or tin cans cut in half. They are light and collect winds very well. Make sure they are big enough to do the job. The smallest cans should be about 6" diameter x 10 to 50 inches long, with at least 6-12 of them. Buy the 6 gallon steel with coating cans (4) from McMaster-Carr for about $10 each. Consider powder cans with 10 gallons for use as wind collectors.

*A very cheap and effective wind collector is a mixing bowl, found as cheap as $5 in a 5 quart size. The ideal design uses standard cast iron or stainless steel woks, about 14 inches in diameter. The rounded outside of the wok never faces the wind. The trick is to connect it to at least one generator, if you run the woks parallel to the ground. Be sure your alternator or generator can handle the extra weight of the woks and handles.

Caveat: Safety is a must, with all of any turbine in a bird cage or ¼ inch screen.

Another major option is to run the wind collectors perpendicular to the ground, with the shaft running two generators instead of one. However the one generator must generate electricity clockwise, and the other generator must generate counterclockwise. The difficulty here involves facing the wind collectors toward the wind in the proper direction. The horizontal collection methods avoids this issue, and mechanics.

Eventually someone will make 4 to 12 plastic turbine collectors that are light and have the shape of the front of a rocket ship. In these cases, be sure the assembly is at least 7 feet above the ground from all moving components, and fully covered with screen.

This is the construction diagram, not the assembly. The reason the central shaft is that the collecting pails will be all facing the same direction, Note the wind direction and fact that the containers or woks face the same direction.

A recent visit to a sustainable community in Hopland, California has inspired a new form of wind turbine. It's made of vertical blinds, about four feet long and about six inches wide. They are curved to the ideal shape of a rocket ship on a pair of round wood or plastic forms.

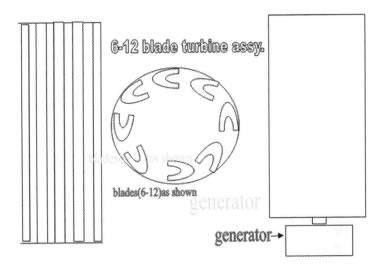

Other options are shown below. Consider 4 to 6 mixing bowls, stainless steel, that can be purchased for $10 each. Other options could include pipes cut in half as seen showing the wind direction below. I used powder scoops on one design that flew off the spindle in heavy winds. Your options are considerable, plus can be inexpensive.

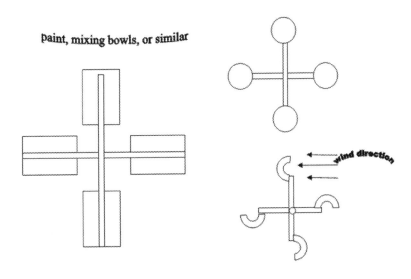

You might want to cut 4-8 paper cups and two wooden stirring sticks and make a prototype first to get the idea of the structure. The cups and wood sticks must be placed so that they are on the side collecting the wind, leaving the other side smooth so the air will flow off the cans easily.

Another option involves using large funnels to power all sorts of small turbines as generators. Take a 3 meter wide by 6 meter high area and make a funnel out of cloth, wood, or any convenient material. For that matter, use the sides of your home and let the generator be at the end. The sides of your home will funnel the wind. I have tried this, and ended up blowing the turbine off it's support.

This method in the city would be ideal in between buildings at any height. You will notice that in narrow alleys, the wind can be powerful.

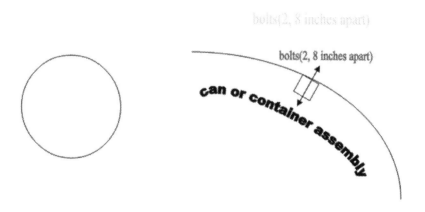

Consider using a bicycle wheel holding mixing bowls or powder scoops with a sprocket to run a 1725 RPM alternator or generator.

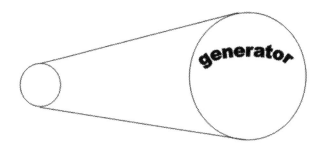

This design also allows you to use the bicycle wheel edge to run the generator without the chains and sprocket.

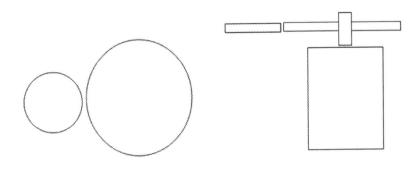

Simple Solar Installations You Can Do

Many options are considered and suggested for inexpensive energy.

*The first would be to use one or more upside down gables on a roof to hold 5 panels, 10 panels, or more. The flat roof is the least effective. Have or build from two to five gables to hold panels from two to five different angles. Ideal angles would be thirty degrees, sixty, ninety, sixty, and thirty on the five gabled structure which can be attached to any roof or patio cover or carport.

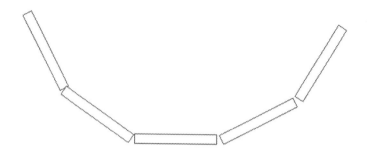

angled, 60 degrees, 30 degrees, 90 degrees, 60, and 30.

You have the panels arranged in an East to West direction so that they always follow the Sun directly. I tested from 7 AM to 6 PM, with fixed panels. The flat roof only gets a third of the solar energy as the ones facing the Sun at all times. This allows you to use a half or third or the typical number of solar panels for the same amount of power. You can set moveable panels anywhere, ground up.

Another method if you choose a flat roof is to have the panels attached to hydraulic tubes and moved facing the sun from daybreak to sunset. You can see that four moveable tubes could move the panels using a timed clockwork system tied into the tubes. Note optional swivel, tool.

Support options for panels are endless. If two 3x5 foot panels are on a 3 x 10 foot plywood base, you can use a pipe with posts at the end to allow the panels to rotate toward the Sun, and be portable. Place any support away from walls, trees, bushes, and potential shade. You can find many places in a yard or on a roof. Another advantage of ground supports allows you to keep the panels out of the wind and clean them easily. Keep them out of the shade of trees or structures. Keep them fenced if possible.

Curved Concave Collection

The best way to maximize optimize output with no tracking system would be to emulate satellite dish antennas. Put 3 or more panels in a 8-16 foot diameter satellite antenna. The panels are at 30 degree angles in most cases. Use at least 5 different angles, from 20 to 30 degrees difference each. I tested 3 small panels and observed better than triple the output of each one.

If you can move 5 panels, put them in a 12 by 5 foot curve and make them face the sun all day. You will eliminate issues of the Earth's Precession.

With the Earth's Precession (movement at poles) at 46 to 47 degrees every year for 30 degrees latitude, you will be moving the panels about once a week to face the Sun. If you use a swivel, consider a clock movement that moves without expensive computerized circuitry. The pipe bases must be moveable too. Below are shown 3 bottom panels at 20 degree angles.

Caveat: Do not use more than 2 panels per assembly. Just make two or more assemblies of 2 panels each to reduce size and wind resistance issues.

If you need more than three panels, make these supports for each 6 x 5 foot module. For 5 sets of 3 x 5 foot panels, weights can vary from 80 pounds each x 5 sets, or about 400 pounds plus frames and attachments. Make the supports handle this and wind-related issues in your area.

The more people that use these ideas, the more your local hardware store will supply options making the installation and operation cost-effective.

Check out swap meets, garage sales, and thrift stores to save money.

Oversized Hammock with 3 Solar Panels on Two Poles 12' high

Instead of getting your suntan on a hammock, find one in the open to hold three 3x5 foot solar panels. Attach the panels on the hammock and the ends of the hammock on poles at least 12 foot high. Make the angles, 45, 90, and 45 degrees for the three panels.

The sides can be held by a cable attached to the center and secured to the ground. This cable could be used to move the panels to face the Sun at least once per month. If you are a little more mechanically inclined, put a pulley on the cable and move the panels to face the Sun more often.

Some hammocks are built so well as to allow the ends to hold the solar panels by themselves. You want the two end panels to hang at 45 degree angles from the perpendicular line facing the Sun. The lower panel is 90 degrees, and faces directly toward the Sun at all times.

Heavy Duty Option of 7 Panels with I-Beams and strong cables

Another option would only require two strong cables strung in between the two poles, with panels attached securely to I beams and each other. In any case, be sure the poles are put in concrete and a two-foot deep Sonotube each.

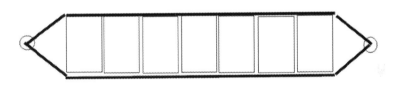

Only the top four feet of the poles are shown above. You want at least 8 feet of pole above the bottom panels facing the Sun. Note that the three panels facing the sun could have the smaller cable and possibly pulley attached to these three sections.

Every month, test the amperage output while facing the whole assembly towards the Sun. You want as high current possible on the meter. Another option might be to have a small electric motor attached to the side cable and pulley to move the unit automatically. The system must handle high winds.

Battery and Energy Storage Issues

Being in rural areas and possibly separated from electrical and gas lines can be a problem. What do you do when there's little sun or wind to power your home and stuff? The self-reliant consumer uses powerful batteries. You may not want to depend on your local(or non-local) gas station to power a gas generator. Keeping a gas tank is risky and can cause explosions and/or fires.

Try to find three or more 12 volt batteries with 900 to 1400 amp-hour ratings. Use from two car batteries per two-panel assembly. If you have 5 sets, connect them to separate circuit breakers. Never put panels on the same connections that your power company uses. The ideal arrangement is to have two separate systems. Check your power company in your area and see if you can do an off-the-grid system. If you can't, you will have to spend more money to hook the panels to the power grid by a licensed professional.

It would be nice to have a Toyota Prius or Chevy Volt as transportation and emergency power. In cases of extreme heat or cold, staying in your car may save your life. Travel to places with less extreme climates if necessary.

One serious idea of value might be to use a hybrid vehicle as a back-up source of power, and temporary source of air conditioning and heating. Depending on where you live or travel, not being tied down to a gas pump might be the best insurance. Note that batteries are improving every year. You may be able to power your home for a month on batteries alone in the future.

Traveling With Wind and Solar

Solar panels are now so powerful that you could put a few atop the roof of a vehicle in a concave support to generate two or three kilowatts per hour while parking or driving under the sun. You might have to add another battery or two to handle the extra output from panels atop the roof.

In some cases, at home, the concave system could power the electric vehicle at anytime, day or night. It's possible to extend travel distances by hundreds of miles with a good roof and hood top collection system.

Choosing the right solar panels is one of the most critical parts of this strategy. Some collect for two hours in direct sunlight, while others may get 3, 4, or even 5 hours of maximum wattage. Be sure to ask the supplier to validate or even prove the value of the panels they sell you.

Chapter 8

Buying Better Services and Stuff for less

Types of Organizations to Consider

For thirty years, I was in debt, varying from $25,000 to $50,000 owed every year. My tax burden was from $10,000 to $12,000/ year, and kept me from paying off the debts. I often spent $2,000 to $5,000 on interest each year. Think of the nicer lifestyle, and vacations that could have been taken every year.

Each user and consumer is expected to decide what types of organizations are out there to save money, resources, and time, plus to protect themselves. The main idea is to inform you of what risks and benefits you will encounter dealing with certain people and groups. What seems good to some people will be evil with others. Make the decisions for yourself. Trust little to opinions, especially ones not verified by facts.

It would be helpful to hope that some of these organizations make an attempt to be more honest, quality and conformance minded, and beneficial to users and consumers. I feel that good organizations should also be moral, civil, compassionate, kind, just, and pay restitution for any harm(s) done.

In this complex world, what you eat, drink, and breath may affect your health. Where you live and what you drive may determine how safe from harm you'll be. If you smoke, do drugs, consume excess alcohol or pills, how often and severe could your diseases be? What issues involve buying goods and services?

There are recommendations that we make most exchanges beneficial for all people. We also have evil, immoral, and uncivil groups - some bureaucratic, non-profit, religious, special interest, anarchic, to terrorist types.

DEFINITIONS

Revenues: they can be money and financial aspects of people's lives.

Resources: include health, time, property, effort, peace of mind, emotional issues, psychological issues, psychical effects, and anything else of value.

Quality: is the measure of how well, good, and able any good or service is able to meet specifications.

Conformance: is the timing, ease of purchase or contract, handling, packaging, and delivering and receiving of any goods or service.

SOME TYPES TO CONSIDER

Greedy, and Greedier:

We might observe individuals or groups that make their living by sucking revenues and resources out of victims. They may also fail in quality and conformance issues for various reasons. In these cases the values received are none or minimal. The victim(s) may be willing or unwilling. Those people who suffer may not know why they do so. They just know they aren't happy with the process and/or outcomes. Money and time was expended to be poorer and/or harmed in one or more ways.

If "buyer beware" signs had to be posted, get a few hundred. Greed and incompetence(and sometimes hostility) bring unwelcome changes by the thousands. Unsafe vehicles have created thousands of pages of laws and unhappy people. Unfair administration of rules, prohibitions, and regulations create public and personal frustration. Airplanes, trains, and vehicles create toxic noise and atmosphere for people living close to airports, railroad tracks, and roads. Poisons are promoted as good for you. Some industrial processes send many to hospitals. You may run into drugs, pills, foods, and drinks not "your cup of tea". Some services are run to run the customer to ruin or take much money and resources from them. Often these organizations are inefficient, slow, clumsy, and sometimes corrupt. You must avoid paying for most services in advance, all at once.

The G&G-like Person

They may not literally suck blood, but money, time, energy, satisfaction, and often results, instead. Often they harm you in ways beyond just physical. They can emotionally drain you. Your feelings or health can be affected.

Once bitten, twice shy as you should be. I have a saying, "You are forgiven, but not excused". This means that someone hurting you may not deserve a second chance. In some cases when they make amends, restitution, and express sorrow, you may try their goods and services again, hoping for better results. Contracts should be in quarterly installments, not all at once.

Howlers, Yellers, and Angry Entities in a Setting, Event, or group

I've experienced so many girlfriends, clients, businesses, bosses, teachers, sellers, and organizations with one or more persons who yell, scream, bully, threaten, and get so angry. These are some of the most disgusting and stressful times you could ask for.

My first job of about 8 years was so pleasant compared to the next 40 years of work. The owners and managers were both civil and friendly. It spoiled me, as the commute was only one mile too.

I used to say, "I get paid half for enjoying the work I do, and the other half for dealing with people". The next two years changed all that. I worked for a half dozen companies in the fashion industry with deadlines, production issues, cost demands, and other messy details. They had persons who had anger issues too. It, for many years, these ogres made me feel that anger was the norm. I know now that expressed anger, screaming, and hostility are evil and often useless.

Often results are achieved this way, but at what cost? There are many events when people have become sick, and or died because of the stress. I can relate a dozen examples, but won't.

These people will surprise you with their outbursts. If you are planning some interaction in the future, forget it.

If you already established some commitments, try to get out of them peaceably. That may not be easy, but you risk losses in revenues and resources too, if you don't leave in time.

In other cases, reduce your number of interactions or times you visit. Make sure you learn which topics may press their "hot buttons".

In another book, I mention the problems in discussing politics, evolution, religion, sex, obesity, nationalities, abortion, literacy, idiosyncracies, technologies, and yelling. For most early interactions, avoid these topics, and avoid potential hostilities to you.

Responding in like for like behavior rarely works. Listen and leave. Get out of their way. Unless you can be convinced they are sorry for their outburst, it is better to stay away, sometimes forever.

Stubborn, Lethargic, Unresponsive, Obstinate Persons or Groups:

So many people and groups seem like they are walking in a fog, or interact in ways verging on unbelievable. Communication is a real challenge. They say and do things that waste time, money, and resources. Before they do too much damage, changes may need to be made. In other cases, they do too little, and solve few problems, wasting your resources and money.

With so much outsourcing, customer relations become strained if understanding the spoken word becomes difficult at best. I know a few languages and may have to use another to get the message across. Buying something or some service is easier than getting problems resolved. The basic training seems to focus on getting money from the customer, but not many benefits, or what in quality and conformance was owed.

On occasions, I have to call later and see if an order was taken properly. Other events end up in hostility to me and not getting anything or service I want. Some sellers misrepresent an item or not send it at all. These people often take offense if being criticized.

Part of the reason for fewer paper newspapers and magazines existing today involve the delivery persons or organization. In a few cases, papers were delivered while I was on vacation. At other times they were placed in irretrievable locations, like directly under my car. Calling to complain was futile, so no papers are ever welcome at my home.

The internet has it's faults too. Some companies occupy or take over your website and can't be removed at any price. Others want some commitment to buy or use their wares. In some cases, my credit card continued to be debited without my permission. I had to change cards and use one with limited funds.

Lethargic systems are no fun either. It can take from 1 to 90 minutes getting results from a telephone call or some data base. Sometimes I ask if the system is working well. Some of these systemic problems rarely get public exposure, frustrate thousands or millions of people.

The Lethargic and/or Stubborn Person

They may not have glazed – over eyes, but come close. They often mistake and ignore your words. You'll sometimes get some advice or feedback, but rarely appropriate. Dealing with them is like talking to the wall. As a functionary of some sort, their mind is made up. You suffer because of their errors, even if they happen to be nice. If they are hostile, watch out!

Others stick by outmoded or useless criteria or policies. They stand firm and won't compromise. Mistakes are made and slowly resolved, taking months or possibly years. It makes no difference what costs in money, time, and resources you suffer. Change comes slowly and painfully in some cases.

Crisis and emotional opportunists

These are the people or companies that make some or all of their profits from people who suffer from crises, disease, disturbances, destruction, disasters, crimes, wars, and other forms of mayhem.

More subtle forms are people or groups that take advantage of emotional issues dealing with crises. They are the ones who get stuff for free or low costs while impoverishing the people who suffer the disaster. Compare these opportunists from the companies and charity organizations that can help the sufferers get back to the original or normal conditions.

Surprisingly enough, people who enjoy positive emotions are often victimized by others. Sometimes they pay exorbitant fees and prices at wedding, vacation, and historical places for products and services. They may be the ones at locations or on conveyances who end up paying twice or multiple times the value of a product or service. These costs often affect people who are captive audiences, or users of insurance.

The nature of these opportunists

Here's a person who can be nicer than your relatives. They say the right things, and make a habit of getting your trust quickly. Timeshare sales people are adept at this. After all, they may get from $10,000 to $100,000 by being persuasive. Wedding planners can be both nice and creative at getting massive amounts of your resources, time, energy, and money. Vacations are a great opportunity to make you spend more than normal.

Are you suffering a crisis? Your funeral director can be so kindly, yet costly. That $2,000 special could multiply with time and tears. Are you injured in some accident. You have to deal with hospital, transportation, and doctor costs – often beyond belief. If you wonder why so many lawyers thrive, consider what some organizations do, or don't do. You are rarely compensated for time, emotional, psychic, physical, and personal harms.

Toxic, chaotic, and hostile organizations

Some aspects of this organization produce side effects that are toxic. It could be pollution of lakes, rivers, seas, land, or the air. These groups also cause accidents that injure people, either at work or in the public domain. Often output from some process or system creates havoc in nature or cities.

We have to careful to distinguish normal outputs from humans and animals of some materials or gases in their normal living and processes. Likely methods of determining this would be to decide if the smells, air, and natural effects are annoying, abnormal, excessive, or dangerous to health.

Some seemingly toxic materials can be processed to reduce or eliminate the effects. It's possible that coal, oil, natural gas, and mineral extraction methods can be improved. The customers and general marketplace will help reduce these problems. We won't need coercive subsidies to force people and companies to use wind, water, subterranean heat, and solar power when economical. The lower prices will prevail. We will also help reduce global pollution and potential loss of oxygen. We can protect coasts from dramatic sea-level rises. Our oceans will be protected from discarded wastes.

Most travel-related entities have some byproducts or wastes. Where shall they be dumped or discharged? In the 1980's many harbors were dirty. Later when a $5,000/day fine was imposed, the harbors were clean by the early 2000's.

Do we have that level of control over lakes, streams, rivers, on land, underground, and in the oceans? It's likely not, and bound to get worse.

The people who refuse to accept realities

There are all sorts of people who believe we don't have "global warming". The earth for them is about 6,000 years old, and has not changed a bit. The "Fertile Crescent" is now the Sahara Desert. The trees were removed about 4,000 years ago. True facts mean nothing to those who make money from products or services that destroy or defile environments. It makes no difference if solar or wind could electrify their home. They are addicted to getting benefits from any toxic method, which may use coal, oil, gas, and underground resources.

We must find out what kind of crisis will change their minds and habits. We know someone can die in a garage with a vehicle operating with no ventilation. What if our sources of Earth's pure air and ventilation run out? Having populations run about with gas masks does not sound enticing to me.

Benign and Beneficial individuals, groups, and systems

You find this type in the use of vending machines, automatic change and money dispensing devices, and in many fast-food environments. They exchange or often trade money for object(s) and services well.

In most of these cases, there seems to be a pure exchange with mistakes rectified almost instantly. For example, newspapers and magazines from vending devices depend on the customer taking only one copy, and leaving the rest for other buyers. These items are expected to be current, and not old copies, unless offered at discount or for free.

Food or drink in vending machines must be safe, palatable, and meet most customer expectations. Near Chicago, Illinois, I remember getting a hot Canneloni with Garlic Bread for $1.35(1991 price) from a vending machine with taste and quality that rivaled items from a restaurant.

In grocery stores and fast-food environments, the food is served hot or cold or room temperature as required. The trick is to get exactly what you want without some error or annoyance. It's rare to find problems in this area.

The effortless satisfaction of those who provide these services

We take a lot for granted by getting so many items and services with little troubling issues. I'm amazed at how so much stuff comes from machines and devices with few spoiled or rancid items. We have machines devoted to just getting the right drink to you. I am grateful for all the people in restaurants and fast-food places who get things done with no mistakes.

In all the condo and home transactions, I was ready to quit or driven to drink. I've owned 50 cars, and rarely had a satisfying car buying experience.

Surprisingly, I had two mobile home real estate transactions and five timeshares go well, with little trauma or headaches. It just shows that there are people and systems that can make something complicated easy and seamless. It's time to spread the benefits out to many more experiences.

Restorative Organizations

These are people or groups who make life more enjoyable for others. You might find a nice restaurant with great food, ambiance, service, and prices. Those establishments make the experience more enjoyable than merely a purely benign exchange.

Consider a good insurance company that pays on time, the amounts needed or contracted for, with no delays or annoying regulations. These companies are helpful in any type of problem or crisis.

Doctors or specialists of all types are of this genre. It varies from a good dentist to a brain surgeon. They cure or alleviate pain, and optimally put you back in ideal health. I have been fortunate to have a few dentists who were good and delightful. Most of my chiropractors have been exceptional. I wish I could say better of many major medical corporations.

Some companies producing medicines or drugs have items that have no adverse side-effects that cause more problems. One may find some minor issues with the drug, but it does not require using other methods or drugs.

Often you will find groups that help people deal with problems. They offer help, support, food, stuff, and services at little or no cost to low income families and individuals. They help people have good health and comfort.

The effortless satisfaction of those who provide these services – part 2

I knew two nurses with degrees in psychology. Their compassion and sense of humor were epic. Most people can quote experiences from these special people in all fields. It could be some special teacher, mentor, friend, or even acquaintance. I used to get nice letters from people who talked with me for a few minutes about the changes they made in their life. Those people in any domain are to be cherished, rewarded, and promoted. It could be a janitor, street cleaner, or trash disposal person who does simpler jobs well.

Cooperative individuals, organizations, and businesses

This is an odd category. Their largess goes beyond merely a salary or fee for employment or service. It requires the owners to share some benefits or profits with all of their employees, workers, and associates. Their vendors and contractors may also benefit from performance or quality rebates.

Many companies will offer four-day workweeks. Added benefits can come from profit sharing paid every three months as some small percentage of their profits. It could include some production or quality manufacturing incentives. Other things involve subsidized (but not always free) food and beverages. Credit union type financial helps may be part of the mix. A good savings and possibly contribution system helps for retirement. The company may offer stock prices to employees that can help in higher stock prices later. Health plans are partially paid for too.

Compassionate persons and groups

Special persons or groups make money or resources from helping others without demanding much in return. Often charitable organizations and a few businesses conduct this function.

Requests for money or resources, or major profits from other ventures, can finance these services. Often the donations are received because of previous events that brought back a good life for many persons after some disaster.

In other cases, obvious needs in various areas initiate restorative actions. Some places need desks for their schools, toilets and sinks for bathrooms, and purified water to survive.

Contracted and contract services

Don't we enjoy relating our experiences with specialists in home, company, health, beauty, and other services? Hopefully your experiences are all positive. One of the best ways to get good ones is to rely on friends, the internet, and special services that rate performances, past and present. The best successes are ones where past work can be checked and evaluated.

Partial payments for partial successes should be considered in many contracts.

The Realities

It will be obvious that there are a set of hybrids in these categories. Also confusing the issue involves the need for taxes to pay for specialized needs by all of us. What seems to compassionate could involve the collection of money and resources to help your neighbors.

In other cases, rules and regulations can cause some problems that require help from the restorative and compassionate categories. The present drug laws have resulted in incarcerating many people in prisons for long periods of time. There is no good reason for this. Eliminating these penalties will reduce the need for restoration of suffering caused by these pernicious regulations. Eliminating many drug laws will also reduce tax costs by paying for people to administer these so-called laws.

Using these categories can help everyone decide which enterprises or organizations are worth supporting. The idea is to benefit from understanding what scenarios you might face. Look for gains, without losses to you or any person, group, or organization you exchange with.

A Challenging Paradigm: Live Well on $30,000/Year or Less

For years my income has be less than that. My goals have been to live well and travel, visit friends, write books and papers, body surf in the ocean, and enjoy a relatively safe and healthy lifestyle. Doing this has been achieved.

I have resorted to timeshares to travel cheaply. In 2009, I spent $3,800 for a month of travel while driving 7,600 miles. The next year I lost 3 clients for some consulting, but was able to buy 3 timeshares for $500. The next year, a month of travel cost $1,200 plus gas costs (about $150). My average use of timeshares is 5 weeks a year costing about half the earlier costs.

Finding all types of housing, food, energy, furniture, appliance, and electronic gadgets at bargain rates was no easy task. My satellite costs varied from $65 to $16 per month. Presently I spend $30/month for my utilities. I live in Southern California for $600 a month in a mobile home. Those who live in more extreme climates may live there for less.

A one bedroom in many cities will cost $1,500 a month, or $18,000 per year. If you share it (or let someone live and rent the living room), your cost is $9,000. A good business will find way to build a two-bedroom unit that still costs only $1,500/month allowing as many as two to four people to share a place for as little as $5,000/ year per person.

You will find thousands of stores competing with each other for your money, time, and resources. Should you drive 25 miles to save $35 a week on your food? If you spend $5 in gas, you still come out ahead. Done each week, that works out to be $1,500 in yearly savings. Avoid credit card purchases, leaving you with $1,000 to $3,000 in money to be used elsewhere. Make those major purchases by cash from stores that sell for much less than normal.

Get to know at least a half dozen options or stores that can compete for your business. You may find that costs in one place are a third or better than others. Do your homework and enjoy the savings.

Observations Department

In my work at 100 companies, not one person who purchased anything ever chose a discount store. My recommendations were ignored, although I proved that these stores on average saved $3.19 for every dollar spent on a survey of 100 typical choices.

It Is What You Like, not Where You Buy It

Hot Tip Consumers: You don't have to spend lots of money to live as well(or even better) than most millionaires.

Most of the vacations you see advertised for five to ten thousand dollars for a week can be had at a quarter that cost. I traveled for 10 days to New Zealand for $650 air fare, $400 hotel, and $350 food and entertainment and sightseeing costs. For example, there was a $39 fee for 3 days at 12 sights in Auckland, and the bus picked me up at my hotel.

For off-season weekend trips, you can still spend as little as $200 for hotel, tickets to Hearst Castle, and a dinner for two at nearby hotels.

Competition is your friend with most restaurants in many places. You can have a seafood buffet for $8.50 at lunch in Some cities. Try splitting the Calamari Appetizer at some places costing $6 each with bread included. At some fast food places, a good meal (skipping the drinks and getting free water and ice) is $4 or less. Try to find reviews of their healthier choices.

If you drive a vehicle, check out the types of gas that will get you 20% better mileage per gallon. You will have to do the comparisons yourself checking mileage accomplished for 15 gallons.

The Basics Can Cost Less

You should be able to live on $100/month grocery costs while living alone, and $75 per person if there are two people or more in your home. I ignore about 95% of the food choices in a market or discount store. Learn to cook and enjoy the savings. You may eat a TV dinner for $1, five times a month. Making the same items from scratch could cost you half of the $5, especially if they are pasta or potato dishes. Some of the notable exceptions may be TV dinners, often sold for $.80 each on special. Load up on them to save money and time.

Use an inexpensive buffet to load up on some meats, poultry, and fish. At home, skip the meat and look for cheap fish and poultry choices. I stay away from buying hamburger and steaks at a market. Try the ground chicken, pork, fish, or ground turkey instead. Another option would be to find good roasts that could provide a half-dozen meals at $2 each for the protein.

No diet is complete without fresh fruits and vegetables. Check labels to avoid chemicals. Try to find proven organic or at least natural produce. The reason you want fresh, or at least frozen, items involves the enzymes and other minerals and vitamins all processing destroys. Commit to at least two fresh fruits and two vegetables daily. You have a multitude of choices depending on locale, and pick what is in season and tastes the best.

Food combinations are critical. Some surveys claim that the body is best in a slightly alkaline PH (about 7.2). Meats combined with starches should not be eaten without a substantial salad. Better yet, have a meat and salad, or starch and salad at separate meals. Try a banana or celery with peanut butter for an inexpensive snack.

Measure twice and save a lot

$1 for a bag of anything is not great if it's only 3 ounces. That works out to about $5/pound. Keep your costs at $2 per pound for most things with exceptions of proteins. For example that bag of potatoes for $1 works out to be $.20 per pound. The cost of a dozen tortillas for $1 amounts to $.09 each. Look for three pounds of bananas or apples for a dollar. Whenever you buy something, determine the $/pound before you buy it.

Delivery charges can wipe out any good deal. Try to get that pasta or pizza or chicken dinner for less at a nearby place. For example, dinners ordered for home delivery may cost $12. When I pick it up it's about $9 saving me 25% of the cost.

Desserts could be Disaster

Besides the excessive sugar and starches in most desserts, the costs can be shocking too. If it's more than a dollar, skip it. For example a piece of pie for $3 for 4 people each might seem better if one for $4 from a store is bought and shared later. Have the dessert and coffee or tea at home. The few places to splurge on desserts are at buffets. Make up for the times you had to avoid buying them at the buffet instead. Stop at a fast food place for dessert if you have to have one away from home. My favorites are the ice cream cone or three oatmeal cookies or muffin from some places costing a dollar or two.

The day-old shelves are not always too old. At some stores, you can get wonderful pastries for $1 on the discount shelves. Usually you have to find them within a few hours of opening. Again, use the $2/pound guide and be sure you get a 2 pound pie for less than $4. The same goes for cookies, with 18 ounces for $3 at the most.

The Drinks On or Over Me

If most people knew that that $2 drink cost the company serving about $.20 in material costs, they might think twice. For a dozen years coffee at the local shops cost me $1.50 for 12 ounces. Now that they have raised prices, I'll buy a cup every other time and pay $1.50 for a bagel with butter so that the costs average $2.50 per visit. Do not spend more than $2 for your beverage anywhere.

"Junk Mail" is not always so junky or annoying. Use the coupons and specials you find every week to save a lot on food and entertainment costs. If you are selective, those free pieces of mail can save you from $3 to $30/month just for checking them out.

You may notice those so-called two-for-one meal specials require purchase of two drinks. Of course, that $4 or more spent pays for the second entrée. I have rarely, used one of those so-called special coupons. Often there are real savings of 25% just using a $2 discount on $8 worth of food.

Are you obligated to buy more at a place that offers you an unbelievable bargain on your first visit? I don't think so. Remember that they treat this as an introduction, and hope you'll return. If I'm not so enthusiastic about the food, service, and ambiance, they may never see me again. I'm picky, and so you can be too. At Malibu, California, some inexpensive places beat many other options at ten times the cost. The city has at least a half dozen places with nice views of the local people and color. An hour or two for less than $10 can be cheap entertainment. That's why you want to calculate your cost per hour for places of entertainment too. I would have trouble paying $50 for two hours of music, yet we have many places that a ten dollar meal or drink that could offer the same fun.

You may be annoyed about the calculating views of food, drink, and entertainment. It would be nice to not worry about the costs. Life for many includes interesting experiences. That hotel you like costing $400 per night could be manageable with a $40 meal for two instead. There are few laws prohibiting you from spending a day in a nice resort and staying elsewhere. Find free parking, low cost food and drink, and comfortable places to allow you more days in a desired place. If the chairs are free, sit and enjoy the world around you, and celebrate the savings and the people you meet.

Things to enjoy for (almost) FREE

Despite the high cost of gas, some free event may cost only $5 for the carload. If you have a local paper, look for low or no cost events and days to visit museums and places of interest. If you leave your money home, the local malls might be worth visiting, if nothing more for people watching.

The first places to consider:

Library for books and internet
Coffee shop for internet
City centers and places for leisure and low cost events
Local parks and plazas
Galleries and boutiques, especially on special days with free food
Museums on the days they offer visits for free

More Activities That Won't Cost Much

Local schools and colleges with special events, usually low cost
Theatres on free or low cost matinees
Bus travel, especially if you can get a day pass
School or college pools at times when the fees are little or none
Festivals, especially when free
Church events
Main streets in nearby cities that make walking a pleasure
Garage and rummage sales
Art receptions and city walks
Beach parks with amenities
Boating, kayak, surfboard cruising

Sometimes Costlier Events and Places on their Bargain Days or Times

Some expensive places offer bargains often hard to believe, but true

Places like Disney or Universal attractions on promotions

Casinos with special events or free transportation

Events at hotels that cost little to enter and enjoy stuff and food

Don't feel obligated to spend money for things offered for free. You may live near places continually offering free art receptions with food, drink, music, and interesting people. Remember that there are wealthy people who make purchases that allow you to enjoy the few hours there for free.

If you go to these places, try to dress to fit in. Cleanliness is a must and you should not smell bad or wear too strong of cologne or perfume. Pay attention to what you see and hear. Be appreciative of what you see or hear. You may be next to the artist or musician, so don't criticize anything too much. Be tolerant and try to understand what the innovator or creator is trying to explain or communicate to the audience. Some art or music may seem repulsive to you, yet we are fortunate to have relatively free speech, not previously allowed in many eras or civilizations.

Expand Your World and Open Your Mind

Our world is changing, and the new paradigm is getting more stuff, resources, and time for less. Salaries and earnings seem to be dropping faster than we can track them. At this point, tax reforms and other options look bleak. The idea is to adapt by supporting people, places, and businesses that offer item and services for much less than we'd normally pay.

You may have to leave the place you live to get a better life. It might mean your friends are a few miles, or hundreds of miles away. You might have to decide if a few visits a year to see people you like will allow you the chance to live comfortably or well in a new area and home. Try to find friendly people, a more civil area, and costs within reason. Malibu may be very costly, while 15 miles away, Agoura Hills or Thousand Oaks could provide options with lower rents and prices on all you need or desire.

Budgeting for the extremes may also be worth considering. What about a place in Central America or Greece? You may find some places like Nicaragua and the island of Kos, Greece very economical. Some TV specials about Ecuador sound good too. The rents and costs of living are low, and the people seem friendly. You might want to learn Spanish, too.

Chapter 9

As that famous dog says "Taking a Bite out of Crime"

If you pay taxes, a quarter of them are spent for crimes and wars

The worst part of crime is that the victims are rarely compensated for their stress, time, annoyances, resources, and getting back to their normal routines. If the criminals were made to pay ten times and/or be sent to separate places without taxes spent, we'd have less crime.

Meanwhile, you'll have to protect yourself in ways that don't require guns, cannons, or bombs. Taking the bite may require you to avoid being bitten in the first place. In most cases, a few things you do to prevent suffering may save your life and sanity. No sense being paranoid or fearful most of your days, as some people endure.

Picking A Safe Place

Do you work in the middle of some large town or city? It's often worth commuting from a safer place. Despite the waste of time to get there, you'll be happier about the place you enjoy. The first thing to do is to find out the crime statistics and rates in anyplace you choose to occupy and enjoy. Do not ignore this step, or you could find yourself continually worrying about which type of crime you will suffer.

There's a reason homes on busy streets cost less. They risk accidents from cars going off the road. Living there can make it easy for a burglar to hit and run quickly. You would do better to be on a cul-de-sac or in a gated community. These are not trivial issues. Find a smaller home or apartment which offers better protection.

In that case, also consider the benefits of a second or higher story unit in a condominium, apartment, or town house. Another option is to pick a place that doesn't seem like is has people with a lot of money. A mobile home park might work, depending on who lives in the park. The desert can be uncrowded, yet in some places still suffer from lots of bad people. There are places in Southern California more dangerous than the inner cities. Do your homework before moving. Check sheriff or police blotters in local papers if you can. Check the internet and drive around the area to get some idea of where you will live.

A Mighty Fortress You Can Have

Not too many thieves like to saw though walls or deal with unbreakable windows. A trick tried by criminals is to throw a stone, break the window, and hope no one is home. Put a quarter (and no less in thickness) inch polycarbonate panels as windows if you want to avoid these problems.

Other options involve planting cactus near windows, or placing a piano, organ, bookcase, or other heavy object to cover some windows. I have two dozen windows in my home, and have most of them covered. Plantation shutters can be great for protection and reducing heat or cold losses in air conditioning too.

You must keep everything locked while you are away in most neighborhoods. Don't trust the kindness or strangers or neighbors. There are so many transients who love to find unguarded places to steal and create mayhem. Make it an unconscious habit to lock everything while gone.

Fancy Can Breed Fear

That desire for water falls, statuary, expensive brickwork, and elegant fixtures could attract theft. If you live in Beverly Hills, California, most homes are elegant and they all have to have extensive protection. Some areas may need private security and alarm systems par excellence.

In a low-crime area, a sign showing that you have a guard dog or special alarm service may attract thieves. Be observant of your neighborhood. Make your protections unnoticeable by anyone.

Chapter 10

Incentives to Make Exchanges Civil, Cordial, and Considerate

Your friends may be the ones who save your life, health, and sanity. If a doctor, counselor, or business keeps you alive, healthy, and happy, you owe a lot to them. Some of the cheapest ways to be happy is to be appreciative and grateful for the benefits you get from many people. It's sad that more people are ecstatic with an officer who let's you off of a violation of some artificial law than those who save your life. We have our values skewed as to which are the right priorities.

Personally, I believe the grocer who sells and promotes healthy foods to keep you out of the hospital is just as important as the doctor who fixes you. I know someone who brushes his teeth 4 times a day and has never had a cavity. On the other hand I've had over 100 cavities found, fixed, and re-fixed again. I attended two health classes in school, and still never learned how to brush or maintain my teeth.

Becoming Aware of Who and What Makes Your Life Better

Most people spend their money, time, and resources on people and things that cause them annoyances and harm. You would find that odd in a society that seems to relatively free. Freedom has it's risks too.

Fewer Hospitals and Drugs and Vitamin Supplements Needed

Ideally, the right foods would have the vitamins, minerals, and enzymes needed to keep you healthy. A hundred years ago, you could find places where people lived to be a hundred years old with just the food they consumed, and the water or liquids they drank. In 1871, a doctor surveyed two communities in the Basque Country. One had people dying before 40 with arterial damage, and the other a few miles away had people living to 80 or more with no heart or arterial issues. The reason to him was the water.

It's really odd that we pay more attention to the coercive and violent programs and beliefs that can make our lives miserable. Reality and news are bad enough, yet we add a multitude of hostile media to make us think that arguments, anger, and maliciousness are the norm. Years back, there was an aphorism, GIGO, Garbage In, Garbage Out. We ignore that to our peril. You would be surprised at how many thousands of dollars you pay yearly for criminal and war-like behavior.

If you haven't been to a thrift store or garage sale, you've missed out on the really delightful exchanges left to us. Recently I received 100 tiles worth $200 for $7, all that I had left in my wallet. Besides that two people loaded them into my car with a bag of concrete. You may not win the lottery, but this is almost as delightful.

With tax system, you cannot afford to waste money on "broken windows". This means, as Frederick Bastiat wrote in the 19th century, people think disasters and wars are good for business. What they don't see is that the other businesses suffer. Your money for travel, a nice meal out, weekend trips, healthy food, and physical activities are wiped out by pills, therapies, and remedies.

Here are some alternatives worth remembering

Good food and drink versus time spent with doctors, drugs, and hospitals

An occasional glass or two of wine or liquor versus nightly bouts of alcoholism

Enjoyable food purchases at stores instead of supplements and pills galore

Playing a penny slot machine instead of wiping out hundreds of dollars at gambling tables

Visits to museums and arboretum in addition to hours working on your own plants, trees, and flowers

Going to a lake, stream, river, or beach instead of taking care of dogs, cats, or birds at higher costs on your own

Watching a sunset or sunrise for two hours instead of TV or radio noise

Paying attention to your spouse or lover instead of someone else's

Offering compliments to those who please you and avoiding complaints where possible. If you do have to complain, do it nicely without anger.

The Social Contract is just that: fewer taxes, and Voluntary Exchanges

When you are forced to pay or provide or avoid stuff and services, you will suffer in some way. Compare free parking to the idiotic parking meters. The better alternative is to charge more to park and not fine people if they park too long in some space. I haven't paid for a parking spot in 40 years and have no intention to ever park in one, for any reason. I only support those businesses that have free parking.

Ask yourself which businesses won't suck a lot of your money, resources, and time away from you. Do you really want to sit around 3 hours for your vehicle's oil change or use the business that gets you out in a half hour. I value my spare time at $20/hour, so I don't want to lose $50 just for an oil change. If you have a vehicle maintenance or repair issue, try to get a free car or at least a shuttle. Avoid using a rental a car or waiting hours to have yours fixed.

In some towns or cities, you don't want to build a home under any circumstance. Dealing with the bureaucracy could cost you time and stress at the very least. Do your research before making any move anywhere. Find out what issues you face with the move. Just getting utilities in some places are a major hassle.

There are places where police do a poor job preventing crime. Besides that, they find thousands of ways to give tickets or fines for stupid or minor infractions. Anyplace that has cameras at intersections is suspect. Those cameras have made no improvement in preventing accidents. They just intimidate people and make them fear the major fines if they get stuck in the middle of the intersection and get photographed.

Rating the Vile Villages or Heavenly Havens

Just as Angie's List promises to find you better service providers, we need a list to rate the areas of misery versus delight. The goal is not necessarily to make people leave some vile area, but to encourage the government and managers to make life better in that area. Maybe it requires less corruption in police and governing bodies. It could require most stop lights to be removed with better traffic flows all over the place. Surveillance cameras are needed for crime prevention and damage control. In "victimless crimes" the cameras should be abolished.

Are there a bunch of greedy bastards running a lot of businesses in some locales? These people should be exposed and expected to change their ways, or let the market avoid them, and they leave anyway. Some management styles are anti-customer and anti-employee. These people should be fired.

I've seen poor receptionists slow company revenues. Telephone operations with people who can't speak properly are bound to fail. Salespeople who don't know their products will send people elsewhere. Rude people of all types should find isolated employment, not needing interactions with the public.

Customers should become more proactive. They should complain about poor products and services. Some companies are quick to respond and change. Others who ignore or fool the public do so at their peril. It's up to us to demand enjoyable lives everywhere, and avoid the stinkers.

Anger Versus Indignation

You are wondering how these topics affect your health. To watch TV and deal with people, you'd think that anger is normal, but you would be wrong. As homework, I highly recommend reading the whole book of James in the New Testament of The Bible. Read it a half dozen times, as it's short with only five chapters.

A lot of people do malicious, ignorant, or stupid things. In these cases, you have a right to be indignant. However, take it from someone who has tried it both ways – avoid anger and hostility as much as you can. I have found it better to be nice and ask for a fix in whatever ails the transaction. Don't resort to being haughty or hostile. You will get more results, and be happy.

Chapter 11

Making Work Plentiful and Palatable

Complaint Department:

On January 11, 1899, The Pemberton Mills had a fire that killed and maimed hundreds of people, most of them women. It shocked the world. What resulted from this disaster were thousands of rules and regulations and laws to protect workers from harm. With 7 billion people and their needs for survival, we still kill millions in work-related disasters, accidents, and toxic environments. In the U.S.A. alone, it is estimated that there are 40,000 injuries in the poultry industries. World-wide mining operations likely harm at least a million people yearly. The list goes on, but we will stop here and suggest solutions instead.

Creative Work Methods and Environments

In my 35 years of management consulting, the employees wanted useful work, good pay, and some useful benefits:

Paying profit sharing every 3 months a percentage of the profit that the company enjoys.

A four day, 9 hour per day work week with guarantees of 3 day weekends at least 25 weekends a year

A credit union, using the L.A.P.F.C.U. (Los Angeles Police Federal Credit Union – I belong to it as my father was a policeman) model.

Annuities at good rates with little risk and loss of capital and earnings.

Group benefits of medical and health maintenance costs and disease prevention, and cures with few or no side effects.

Managers that are moral, civil, cordial, and considerate

Work rules, policies, and conditions that are reasonable and safe

Subsidized food and beverages at breaks and lunch

Group purchase opportunities of food, groceries, and other products of value

Potlucks, parties, and group activities that make the organization fun

The above list suggests some of the basics rarely seen in many organizations. Often one or two of the above are tried or in practice. All of these are good things to have in all organizations.

Time For An Automation Department

In the 1940's cotton picking and processing was automated. Earlier, in 1818, The Niles Register documents a 330,000 person savings with the Whitney Cotton Gin. Why haven't we automated every other grown product from the Earth?

In the strawberry fields, you will still see masses of people, probably straining their backs, picking them. In 1979, I previewed optical devices and developed $5,000 robots that would have made the process automated. The optical device cost $30,000, but in mass production, it would have cost $9.000 or less. Much to my parent's annoyance, I used to shake their grapefruit trees to collect the fruit. Work-related activities can be automated.

Smoke and Mirrors

Many entrepreneurs ought to look in a mirror and ask why they make their workplace so toxic. I remember a place in Spain where the person was covered in black grinding and polishing metal utensils and art objects. If not automated, why didn't the person have a vacuum to remove the dust and debris?

Much of the need for medical help could be alleviated by safer and cleaner work environments. It's no coincidence that outdoor work like landscaping and delivery jobs are more enjoyed than other occupations. Although it would be better if the "mow and blow" were mow and vacuum, life outdoors in many places is safer than an office, airplane, or factory.

Most buildings foster foul air. They don't have skylights, open windows, or air purifiers. You would need all three in places where dust, desert, and pollen could cause allergic or disease reactions to the air. In 1992, I determined that a move from Carlsbad, California to the East Coast for Hughes Aerospace would add a cost of $100,000 a year for air conditioning. They changed their strategy and moved to Marietta, Georgia instead.

Liquid Gold and Waste

Why are some sources of water not fit to drink. It's as if the 17th century of drinking wine, beer, and spirits were still needed. Instead we pay billions for bottled water. What did we do to destroy the water sources and places? It would take a few volumes to explain why.

There are some places where it's safe to drink the tap water. With our added populations it will take wind and solar energies coupled with devices to purify what's left. We must rethink and implement new technologies to produce all products soon. Although steel, copper, gold, marble, and other materials are plentiful, plant and tree alternatives must be offered soon.

Composite must become the silica and glass of today.

Nuclear, Oil, Gas, and Mining Alternatives

In the 19th century, people were proud to be covered with oil from a productive well. A few million people suffered during the gold rushes. Few of those people made worthwhile wealth. In our haste to get natural gas, we already pollute some water and ground areas. Mention Five Mile Island and Chernobyl, and you know the rest.

Some Energy Sources Will be Gone Sooner Than You Can Imagine

The first oil well gushed in 1859. The last ones will give out 200 years later. It's later than you think. Digging up provinces in Canada won't last long, especially if our population increases to 10 billions soon.

Here's a few alternatives we can use now

Wind power in Western Oklahoma could power the Midwest U.S.A.

Solar power in sunny areas could power the whole state and beyond

There's enough geothermal energy near Yellowstone to prevent a major explosion and power the Northwest.

Bicycle generators can be used in places not choosing the above methods.

We have a flashlight that runs a half hour on a minute's work so someone on a bike could power a whole home.

Miniature TV's, radios, telephones, computers, and other devices will cut power consumption by 90 percent or more.

Plant and other wastes are already used to power some factories and offices.

More effective motor technologies will make cars, trucks, and robots much more economical to run.

Housing will be designed to make air conditions costs reasonable at any local temperature, humidity, and wind condition.

Jobs Galore (trading material for labor costs)

I saw a half pound of Starbuck's Coffee from Guatemala selling for $12/half pound. The same weight in oil goes for about ten cents. Coupled with a 4 day, 9 hour a day work week, few would go unemployed or live in poverty with different forms of work to do.

The world seems to be to get more of the basic needs at lower costs. If we are paying someone $.30 instead of $30/hour, the cost of that item should be less. That's why designers of automated devices are hoping to be competitive with those lower salaries in more expensive places.

After maintenance and repairs, a machine won't ask for a salary raise or need hours for breaks, or personal, sick, and vacation time off. Yet those same devices need people to design, install, repair, maintain, and fix them.

If farmers choose more valuable produce, they can afford more people to work with machines to help them grow, harvest, and transport whatever they choose to sell. Classic examples involve all sorts of liquor and spirits. Wine-growing can be profitable for small producers, as with those in the Champagne District of France with thousands of private vineyards. The same goes for all other types of liquors.

Coal, gas, and oil supplies are not renewable. Trees and plants can be renewed as long as the soil is kept productive with ample water and nutrients. Henry Ford and George Washington Carver had planned to make their vehicles from purely farmed materials until Mr. Carver died, and the ideas went with him.

In Honduras I got a ride to the coast with a person who had a large farm of coconuts. He used the husks and waste materials to make 40 different products until the government seized his business. Just look at all the tree and plant trimmings to visualize products made from them. Millions of people will have work when the chemists get busy designing products from those presently discarded leaves, stems, and husks.

Letting the "we versus they" (employees versus management.) Profit sharing paid every three months, equally to each employee, takes away much of the conflict.

To prevent abuses of any benefit, a shared cost works best. Offering low cost lunches makes more sense than free ones. Those who don't want the lunches won't abuse the option.

One successful event involves a free meal with a celebration offered for those departments in manufacturing or processing who do not have an accident in a month or three months. In various companies, I instituted this event which cost $1,000/year (for 450 people) and saved $250,000 dollars or more yearly on accident costs.

There is a myth implying managers have to be aggressive and cold to get results. It has been proven that the civil and nice methods get from 15 to 40 percent more output. At "month – end madness", I managed shipping departments which shipped 3 times the normal amount in a days' time.

Most people can't afford a home or vehicle on a cash basis. Credit unions are the best form of union to save money and allow people to live some of their dreams. If the future paradigm is to live well on less money and resources, we do better with helpful institutions for finances and purchases.

A Purchase and Service Based Economy

A balance is sought here. If people must work to get stuff and services, we need to offer them time enough to enjoy these benefits. That is why it is likely most people will work only 4 days a week so they can pursue personal goals while helping others to profit from the visualization, plans, and accomplishment of the dreams. In 60 companies I consulted, I eliminated all overtime in 65 out of 70 of them.

Your exceptions may require stocking and maintenance by part-time personnel for 6 hours/day. The goal is to limit these kind of activities to times that the organization is closed. For two nine-hour day jobs, that could be six hours at night. Avoiding customer interactions is to be desired.

Chapter 12

Disannoying The Cities

Your best friends won't tell you, but many cities have their areas of disaster, not from nature, but poor design and poverty. There are places you wouldn't send your worst enemy to. I'm not taking names and calling others about the problems. If your city, county, or parish council members are so blind, maybe it's time for a private management company to take over the work.

Gentrification, or Just Relocating the Poverty-Stricken?

A friend of mine lost some land in Central America because many criminals were exported to the area he owned. Instead of a quiet and private spot on a lake, he got demands to build walls and protect his homestead from thousands of miles away.

Do you recall the last chapter suggesting that water features be put in every area possible? For existing lakes or streams, they already command a price and benefits. Ocean-front places are already priced out of most people's budgets. In some areas, the lake or river front property gets the top dollar too. The canals in Venice, California, are so expensive, that most of the poor now commute by bus or car, and contract for work from the wealthy.

I've spent time in large cities in over 50 countries. Often, kind strangers would tell me to avoid certain areas as dangerous for me. Since I look like a kind lending agent, they had no problem detecting me as the foreigner.

Many places have many lakes and ponds in their vicinity. Look for them as places to enjoy or live in. Most people would enjoy water features close by.

Nature Reclaims It's Territory

If you visit ancient ruins, you will learn that the trees and bushes may have overrun what was originally desolate landscape. One hypothesis claims that the Mayans and Aztecs decimated their tree population to cover the buildings with limestone. This was done to make their buildings look nicer. Others believe that the religious leaders demanded buildings that would impress the people. Who cared about the lack of food or greenery it created?

Some cities have already set aside a percentage of space for parks, trees, bushes, and growing gardens for food. Considering how little space is needed to grow food, making the farmer's market a permanent part of the town seems to be a good idea.

Most apartment or condominium complexes have open space that can be used to grow food. Those areas should be maintained by the management and food offered at reasonable costs to those who desire locally grown stuff.

Make sure the food is pest and chemical free. At certain times, netting should be used to keep birds and insects away from the ripe food. You don't want to share the bounty with other animals or insects.

Shade is a good thing to have in areas that are hot. My Oleander bush keeps my home from five to ten degrees cooler in the summer. How do I know that? When it was trimmed in 2010, the interior in my home required external air conditioning half the time. The next year, the need dropped in half when the bush grew out. When my parents cut down their Mulberry Tree, the home became so hot. They were forced to buy 3 air conditioners without the shade this large tree provided.

Cactus and other sharp plants look great, and can protect windows from criminals naturally. The ground floors are the most vulnerable to theft, so these plant cops can save the day and the stuff. They might just save your life.

Reducing the Effects of Overcrowding

The idea of celebrating New Year's in Times Square has always been repulsive to me. I used to go to music concerts with a few thousand people, but those days were over 20 years ago. Fortunately many cities provide great entertainment for a couple thousand people in more intimate settings. The Dorothy Chandler Pavilion and Disney Performing Arts Center are two enjoyable places, much smaller than the Collisseum nearby.

In recent years, traffic in LA's downtown has been reduced – possibly by high gas prices. There are more people living in LA, but it seems less congested than 20 years ago. The traffic misery has moved to the suburbs. Thousand Oaks traffic and the lights can make a two mile journey last 15 minutes. My trip to the swimming pool at California Lutheran University takes from 7 to 22 minutes, depending on how long I wait at the 18 lights.

I'm not sure how money is spent on traffic controls and accidents in most cities. It's likely that the wastes of money could be reduced by roundabouts and over and underpasses on the main roads. You would think that free shuttles on main thoroughfares would be the norm in all cities. Think again. Considering that the New York Times has fully automated its movement of paper rolls, the same could be done to transport people in the main streets of the large cities. No such luck or efforts are to be found. The priorities of many bureaucracies are time-wasting at best.

Congestion is also bad for the air. The typical vehicle emits about a half pound of carbon dioxide every minute. If your car sits at lights for a half hour, you emitted as much as 15 pounds into the atmosphere, in just that time you drove. Some vehicles are nearly zero, and other will spout out a pound a minute.

No amount of fancy stuff in a vehicle is going to alleviate the stress of gridlocked traffic of people and vehicles. At some time in our future, we will have to address things that anger people. Much of the rudeness and hostility comes from waiting in lines, vehicles, or for public transit.

Noisy Can Be Nasty

What and where are the places of poverty? Try railroad tracks, truck lanes, factories, some bars and discos too close, for starters. Your next door neighbor's stereo could be too close for comfort. I moved about 20 times out of the 50 because of rude and noisy neighbors. One ocean and park-view place was vacated because of noisy bar patrons making noise at closing time.

On a trip from Washington D.C., I saw dozens of miles of vacated places next to the railroad tracks in 1991. What could have been the reasons? Try living next to a track and decide for yourself. These days, the railroad conductors love to honk their horns at all hours of the night, waking most people up. Maybe in 1870 this was a pleasure, but these days, it must contribute to crime, annoyances, and low real estate prices nearby.

I lived near a neighbor whose bird sounded worse than fingernails scraping on a chalkboard. There was nothing to do to sound-proof my place. Just putting in triple-pane windows and doors would have been useless.

In Redondo Beach, some motorcycle riders loved to cruise the Esplanade at 3:30 AM dozens of times, making massive amounts of noise. As you well know, there are laws prohibiting noisy vehicles. None of them are enforced.

A civil society, if ever practiced, will include less noise, especially between 11 PM and 7 AM to allow people to get 8 hours of uninterrupted sleep. My apologies to the trash truck drivers who will have to start work one or two hours later. Maybe the management will install air conditioning making work all day comfortable.

One has to ask why police, fire, and emergency vehicles run their sirens while the roads are empty. For people driving the opposite side of the road, these noise-makers are worthless anyway. Has anyone made surveys of how effective noise is to prevent accidents or get a patient to the hospital any faster? The roads are so congested, getting an extra minute seems unlikely.

Paying for and Preserving the Quiet Pleasures

Must we have all 24 hours in a day to make all the noise we want? This should be a fundamental question in all places. If there's a noisy factory or place of work, maybe we could use the 11-7 noise curfew for maintenance or other quieter activities. The side-benefits could be lower energy and overhead costs. In addition, many factory workers might prefer to work four-eight hour days to avoid the stress and monotony of their jobs. I worked in 70 manufacturing facilities, and rarely did I find anyone who wouldn't like reasonable compensation and 4 day work-weeks.

Most railroad tracks should be placed in the middle of the freeways where noise is a 24 hour guarantee. Fortunately, some places have sound-walls to reduce the annoyances. For example, the Trains in Florida would best be placed along the 75, 95, and 4 Freeways, not in the middle of cities.

The railroads should have two tracks and overhead and underground (preferably) tracks avoiding the need for signals, gates, and the resulting accidents they guarantee.

It's obvious that most elevators, moving sidewalks, and escalators are very quiet. For ease of movements in the crowded area, there should be more of these way to travel, reducing the need for cars, busses, railroads, bicycles, and costly transport options.

Chapter 13

Protecting the Coastlines

Will a Tsunami or 6 – 11 meter(about 20-40 feet high) storm surge be coming to your area? You might be surprised at which areas are at risk. You've seen some of those documentaries on TV. Eventually, you may have to be scared into some real action. Yes, it's time to think about coastal protection.

A Wall You Can Live and See With

I spent 25 years and a quarter million dollars of my time and money traveling to 50 countries and thousands of beaches. I stopped at many places and offered short essays or a lecture. So far, just a few reefs have been built, but most not for protection.

More recently, it seemed to me that a small pair of walls of tubes sticking about 4 foot from the ground would help a lot of vulnerable cities and coasts.

Unfortunately, the posts may have to be sunk 50 feet deep with 4 feet sticking out above the ground. Two rows of these are needed about 5 feet apart to store tubes that go over the posts in case of major storms. For most cities, this would be adequate protection. Just make sure your power and other utilities are located at least a hundred feet higher than your coastline. Don't make the same mistakes made in Japan. They thought their 30 foot walls would save them. They were totally wrong.

The two walls will store 20 to 30 foot high tubes in between the walls. The tubes would be pulled out in cases of emergency to make a pair of tall walls to keep much of the water out of your town. You don't want to deal with the aftermath, such as the folks have done in Texas for 100 or more years.

The goal is to provide tube storage making sure your tubes don't rust if you use steel, and keep them from getting too much sand or dirt on them. They should always be ready for some high storm surge, up to 30 feet in height.

One problem involves access to the beach. You can build stairs over the walls or leave an opening. However that opening must be closed, or your problem will worsen with strong streams of water going into your town. Handicap access could be done on level ground or with a device able to lift people up and over the two walls (something like a crane with pulleys).

The first thing you will have to do before the storm and waves reach the wall is to get everyone except the emergency personnel away from the coast. Placing those tubes in heavy winds may be no easy task. It's better than spending billions of dollars of repairs and injured people later.

There are two more sophisticated methods of protecting coastlines. They are more expensive, risky, and passive. You can see both types in a few coasts, and they are listed for your information if you want to try all aspects of protection instead of leaving town.

Offshore Breakwaters Save Coasts from Big Waves

If you live near Venice, California, you can see the local offshore breakwater providing protection and surf options for recreation. They were tried near the Santa Monica Pier, but were destroyed by the 1980's from large waves and too light of stones laid down in 1938.

The typical breakwater is about 100 meters long with 3 to 10 meter wide stacks of 15 to 20 ton boulders. They should be at least 6 meters high.

Offshore Artificial Protective Reefs – Complicated But Worth Trying

An attempt was made at El Segundo, California, to use sand bags to build a protective reef. Unfortunately it was placed in water too deep and next to a coastal concrete reef that sucked up most of the waves.

If you have a lot of 20 ton stones nearby, this could be a viable option for a vulnerable coast. It's just the very first step in a multiple step program to protect any coast.

These structures are similar to the breakwaters, so they will be shown together with them and their own design. Both types of structures can be used. In most cases, all structures are of little use in Tsunamis more than 10 meters high. Yet I am convinced that putting these items in place would improve the chances of saving lives and property.

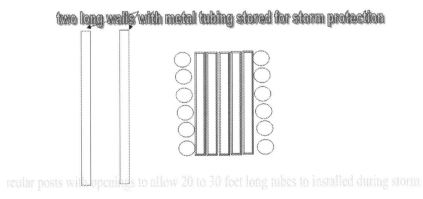

Circular posts with openings to allow 20 to 30 feet long tubes to installed during storms or Tsunami

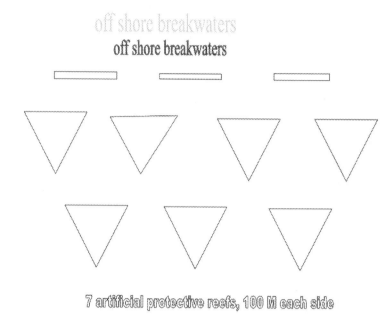

off shore breakwaters

7 artificial protective reefs, 100 M each side

A Comprehensive Plan Protecting Any Coastline

You start from water less than 40 feet or 10 meters deep and work forward toward the coastal features. The above top view shows ten structures that could protect about ½ mile to a kilometer of coastline (about 2,500 feet or so).

These are not inexpensive, but you might question how much damage another Tsunami or storm surge could cost. Most people don't realize that Ventura, California, had one in 1818. Back then, a hundred thousand people, mostly missionaries and local Indian tribes, occupied the area. Now, a similar event might cost the area 100,000,000,000 dollars (a hundred billion). Costs to protect the area would be likely 5 billion dollars or less. It would depend on how cheap and accessible the stones can be, and what labor and machine costs are required to build the reefs.

At the very least, the whole coastline from Point Mugu to Emma Wood State Park should be protected. This would be a good project for the CSCI (California State College at Channel Islands) to design if they have instructors and classes in oceanography.

Other Coastal Features to Consider

Many places already have rock revetments, or large stones placed in front of the homes on the shore. For waves up to 6 meters, these could be the cheap way to provide protection. Access to the beach is provided by stairs made of concrete, such as they did in Malibu.

Some coasts have more area in front of sand or pebbles, often dry at low tides. You will see natural dunes made of sand and lowly plant cover like ice plant and other hardy varieties. In some places, these should be planted as the first option to protect homes behind them.

In summary, here are some coastal protection options:

Indestructible housing with infrastructure located in protected places
At least 4 foot high wall of iron reinforced brick at the property end
Two 4 foot high walls of posts with space for 20 – 30 foot tubes
Bushes and ground cover in front of the posts and tube area
Underwater offshore breakwaters, 100 meters long, spaced 50 meters
Above water offshore breakwaters, at least 6 meters high
Artificial protective reefs, at least 7 with 100 yard sides of 20 ton rock

A Side View of the Options

structure .. wall .. posts/tubes..plants..underwater breakwater/reefs

The areas where normal wave action occurs are the most difficult in design. An approximate formula developed by D.D. Gaillard in 1902 was 1.42 to 1, the depth of water to the wave height ratio. You want to have protection for a 6 meter high wave, so the water, at the least depth would be 9 meters. We also want to protect for 10 meter high waves, so the rear portion away from shore would be 14 meters high. These offshore structures should number at least 7 to 10 for every half mile of protection. They aren't cheap, but better than doing nothing.

As you can see, life is not so easy for people on the coast. As time passes, you may find that fewer homes will remain, and beaches will make better business and pleasure for everyone because of the rarity of the coastline frontage. The beaches that are left may need walls and reefs to avoid sea level rises and storm issues in the future.

Chapter 14

Profitable National Parks

The Governator's Complaints Almost Realized

A few years ago, many state parks were slated for closure. Fortunately the public outcry kept most of them open. As a form of therapy, all state and national parks must be maintained for public use. Many of these places are not replaceable without massive expense. Case in point can be pointed to the LA Red Cars, removed in the 1960's by corrupt people, companies, and bureaucracies.

Gladstone Fish Restaurant Emulated

Take a trip to Sunset Boulevard and PCH(Pacific Coast Highway in California) and stop at Gladstone's. It's been a fixture for decades and the last I heard, has made more than 5 million dollars annually each and every year.

Most parks can emulate this success with adequate parking and good food, ambiance, and service. It's not as easy as it would seem, but worth the effort in all cases.

I'd also throw in a Starbucks or Coffee Bean and Tea Leaf at each locale too.

While we are at it, why not include some fast food place for those who want to avoid tipping and longer stays.

Did you ever wonder why Santa Monica's POP and Long Beach Pike amusement areas lost out? Look at Disney and Universal Studies operations. Space permitting, maybe some attractions could be included, especially a water park in warm areas.

Energy Costs To Be Provided by the Park

Yellowstone is in an area having geothermal energy opportunities. Why not build some facilities that can be hidden among trees to provide power? One risk involves the chance that the whole park may explode, taking the area and resources of the whole state with it. Some research should be done to see if these risks could be reduced by tapping into the heat of the magma and water to provide power for more than a few states.

Invest one percent of the area of the park to save billions of dollars. I'm not suggesting that we convert all of a park to business or energy concerns. It's easy to hide power plants, such as the ones at Niagara Falls. Depending on the energy source, each park could be a prototype for energy provided without using coal, gas, or oil.

As you have read, we can find most energy just above ground as with wind and solar. The ideal underground involves geothermal, taking advantage of conditions we already observe and enjoy. Don't take away the mud pots and heated pools anywhere. Just find ways to bring piping in without impacting the views and enjoyment of the parks.

Chapter 15

Your Choices Count

Democracies in the public and market places

What if the same enthusiasm for sports, leisure, movie and media stars, and vacations worked in the social domain? We need more money, resources, and time spent on things and services to keep our society going. This book was not written as some childhood schoolboy exercise. It's goal is to stimulate action and peaceably made choices to assure our long-term survival.

Don't Say or Read, "that's nice" and do little or nothing

Rather than take names or embarrass people, try these in your own world and reap the benefits yourself, or for our future inhabitants:

Find a vehicle that gets better gas mileage – the oil companies don't need your money as they have profits beyond belief

Go through your home and commit to at least a quarter less expenses for gas, electric, and water utilities

When you replace any appliance, get the one(s) that need less energy and do more than before.

Insist or work on a 4 day, 9 hour a day work week and take 3 days in a row with no overtime. Tell or ask your bosses to do the same.

Demand at city council meetings that they make the roads and lights and tracks safer in your area.

Work with other people to make all parks safer, nicer, and more profitable so there's no incentive to close or limit useful hours.

Install a small wind turbine or solar panel device to charge a car, or do some household energy saving errands.

Paint your outdoor water heater black to collect the sun's heat, or at least put some pipes in the sun to heat your pool.

If you live on a coastline, ask the planners and council how they will protect you in case of some potential disaster. We don't need any more Japanese earthquake and tsunamis to make changes now.

Get your local schools and institutions to design and test homes and structures that can be destroyed by winds, floods, or storm surges.

Instead of occupying or harming private or public places, write letters and politely ask them to change the tax laws and avoid financial crises.

Promise yourself you will channel your anger and hostilities for the many injustices into civil and cordial and competent actions that give incentives to change what needs improvement.

Celebrate changes by rewarding the change agents, designers, planners, and workers who are involved. Give everyone credit for their work.

Track progress using measurement, statistics, and benefits derived at reasonable costs in money, resources, and time expended.

Be grateful for the discoveries, inventions, developments, and changes made in the past that have made life enjoyable for everyone. Read their biographies, watch the documentaries, and pick positive programming to keep your mind open and stimulated.

Chapter 16

Miscellaneous Options

Water Shortages in Your Future?

Just because California has had a flood of rain and water doesn't mean there won't be other dry periods. One is recorded from 1276 to 1296 A.D. forcing the indigenous folks to move North, out of the "Four Corners Area".

So what do you do to conserve water? Using less is an option that may require some inconveniences.

- Take a trip to the Southwest areas of Arizona. You will notice a lot of colored rocks replacing the nice green grass. Factor that into the future.
- Use water faucets which have lower outputs, but faster flows.
- Purchase or ask for subsidized options to install waterless urinals and low gallon commodes.
- Use paper plates and plastic utensils to avoid washing dishes.
- Avoid using mechanical dishwashers unless less than 15 gallons of water required.
- Increase your water collection devices to hold thousands of gallons.
- Put your plants in single lines, eight to ten feet high and use only drip irrigation.
- Plant very low use water types, possibly cactus and semi-arid types of plants that can be enjoyed as food.

- Consider septic tanks, composting toilets, and water purifiers as some of the many portable technologies.
- And somewhat uncomfortably – Store your urine in half gallon widemouth jars and use the urine in powering a daily flush in a commode.

Living in or Near Toxic Areas:

Sometimes you could be stuck next to some place spewing smoke or toxic chemicals. Maybe the river, lake, stream, or even ocean is polluted. What can you do?

- Use and air purifier in you living room, and bedrooms.
- Find an Ozone device to purify your air.
- Get a water purifier if your groundwater tastes bad or has high sediment counts.
- Build a surrounding structure that insulates you. A simple one might use one-inch steel I-Beams, with 3/8 inch thick walls of wood, steel, and/or polycarbonate plastic panels.
- Have windows that can be opened incases of purer air at certain times – possibly automatically.
- Find supplements that you can take to counteract the toxic effects in your area or workplace.
- Get out of town as often as possible. Maybe a timeshare, friend, acquaintance, or place is available to get purer air and water access on a temporary basis.

Being Near or Friends With Positive People:

Does your work, business, exchange, and interactions make you angry or annoyed or stressed?

Try to avoid places or situations that create stress in your life. Some studies are proving that issues like COPD, or Asthmas, or even dementia come from stressful situations. If you are of a sensitive type, you may be more subjected to the negative affects.

In at least two dozen work environments, I had to change jobs much sooner than expected.

In about 50 of the 70 consulted companies I worked in, there was a person who was out to make my life there miserable. I used to say, "My work is fifty percent doing what I love to do, and the other half dealing with people".

Remember that a sustainable lifestyle involves living long enough, in good health, with few disabilities and diseases.

Some situations are accident-prone. They may involve poor safety and hazard efforts. Other places may have more than their share of floods, high winds, earthquakes, and weird weather. Find out where these are and avoid them like the plague.

Pick your vacations, travel, and even group activities with care. Be sure you like the place, weather, warmth, comforts, and facilities before you go there. Don't be the statistic that laments the miserable time you had.

Why do Starbucks now have drive-in places? It's a place to socialize with some risks inside. Other places also have the same risks. Try to avoid people with colds, flu, coughing, sneezing, and other diseases you might pick up. I was infected by a half dozen people in various places from garage sales, to fast food, to airplanes who had Bronchial Pneumonia, and coughed on me.

Pick uncrowded times to enjoy your purchase, service, or transaction. Get through the lines and see the cashier faster. Make sure you don't take too much time in cash, credit card, or other checkout procedures.

The Process Should Be as Enjoyable As the Result(as often as possible):

Dentists use various forms of ways to dull the pain. Make sure that yours does the work easily.

For that matter, make sure you find out, by internet, friend, or referral who and where to get good stuff and service with no stress or annoyances.

Printed in the United States
By Bookmasters